Solo Flight

A Bipolar Odyssey

by

Cynthia Martin

McSeas Books

Address for orders:

McSeas Books
1532 Santa Rosa Ave.
Santa Barbara CA 93109

www.mcseas.com

Copyright © 2007 Cynthia Martin
Second Printing with corrections
Cover design by Peggy Lindt

All rights reserved. No part of this book may be reproduced in any manner whatsoever without written permission from the publisher, except in the case of brief quotations embodied in critical articles or reviews.
– McSeas Books

Printed in the United States of America
Library of Congress Cataloging-in-Publication Data

Martin, Cynthia
Solo Flight: A Bipolar Odyssey

ISBN 978-0-9712827-6-6

USA $16.00

The events of this story are essentially true. In addition to interviews, research, and first-hand observation, I have reconstructed some scenes in which I was not present. Some scenes contain imaginary minor characters who act as a supporting cast to facilitate the action. Dates of past decades may not be precise due to lack of documentation, and the dialogue may not contain exact wording as it was spoken. However, these dates and conversations are as accurate as I can remember.

Some of the people in this book, including the minor characters in reconstructed events, have been given pseudonyms. My brother's writing has been edited only for occasional spelling or punctuation. I have reconstructed his thoughts in only one instance, and the reader is forewarned in that chapter.

—Cynthia Martin, 2007

bipolar disorder, *psychiatry*:
An affective disorder characterized by periods of mania alternating with periods of depression usually interspersed with relatively long intervals of normal mood. Formerly, manic-depressive illness.

Random House Dictionary of the English Language, 2nd Edition

CONTENTS

Introduction — viii

Part I: Witness to Madness
Chapter 1: On a Cuban Beach — 2
Chapter 2: The Nightly News — 5

Part II: The California Dream (1945-1961)
Chapter 3: The San Fernando Valley — 10
Chapter 4: Growing Up — 15
Chapter 5: The Storm — 19

Part III: The Wild West (1961-1964)
Chapter 6: You Wanna Go to Elko? — 30
Chapter 7: Signs of Trouble — 34
Chapter 8: Christmas at the Callahan — 38
Chapter 9: The Phone Call — 43
Chapter 10: Flipping Out — 47

Part IV: Turbulent Years (1965-1988)
Chapter 11: The Shady Rest Motel — 53
Chapter 12: Friends and Family — 57

Chapter 13: Crescent City	60
Chapter 14: Flying Stories	64
Chapter 15: LAX	69
Chapter 16: Trivial Pursuit	73
Chapter 17: Conversions and Conversations	78
Chapter 18: The Mafia	85

Part V: Tilting at Windmills (1989-1999)

Chapter 19: A Spiral of Zeal	90
Chapter 20: Big Brother and STDs	99
Chapter 21: The Wages of Sin	105
Chapter 22: Questionable Sources	110

Part VI: A Lifelong Legacy—Kevin (1985-2003)

Chapter 23: Special Education	120
Chapter 24: Child Protective Services	123
Chapter 25: Family Court	127
Chapter 26: The Rancher's Inn	130
Chapter 27: Paper or Plastic?	132

Part VII: Preface to a Crime (1996-2001)

Chapter 28: The Funeral	138
Chapter 29: The Sirens of Mania	143
Chapter 30: More Adventures of Madness	146
Chapter 31: Return to the Callahan	152

Chapter 32: Preparations in Florida	157

Part VIII: The Fall of Icarus (2001)

Chapter 33: The Headlines	163
Chapter 34: The Pizza Pilot	167
Chapter 35: Repercussions	173
Chapter 36: Aftermath	179

Part IX: A Trail of Madness (June 2003)

Chapter 37: Coming to Terms	186
Chapter 38: Miami Justice	191
Chapter 39: A Personal Legend	198
Chapter 40: Scene of the Crime	201
Chapter 41: Profile of a Felony	205
Chapter 42: Marathon to Key West	214

Part X: Consequences

Chapter 43: Insights	220
Chapter 44: The Visit	224

Epilogue	231
Bibliography	235
Acknowledgments	239

Introduction

I have a recent photo of my brother. His fierce blue eyes penetrate the camera lens. Sun-tipped brown hair splays in chaos over a balding scalp, and years of illness line his skin. This is a face that reflects the terror of madness.

I also have other photos of Milo: as the small tot with the bandaged head; the smiling third-grade birthday boy wearing a paper crown, cheeks expanded, blowing out candles on a slightly askew birthday cake; in his Canoga Park High School football uniform, a cheerleader on either side.

It was a given in our family. We three children would grow up, go to college, and enter professional careers. I became a high school teacher, my sister a college professor. Milo has worked as a ranch hand, carpenter, day laborer, landscaper, van driver, courier, miner, handyman, garbage collector, box boy, worker in a kitty litter factory, and pizza delivery man. His résumé reflects the circumstances of his life, one of repeated episodes of debilitating manic-depressive illness.

Throughout decades of poverty resulting from his manic episodes, Milo has learned the tricks of survival on the streets of Reno and other cities. He discovers the Salvation Army thrift stores, street corners to wait for day-labor jobs, the nearest Western Union.

"I never pay at the food fair in Miami," Milo told me after one of his trips to Florida. "I just go from counter to counter for the free samples."

Milo also visits department store cosmetic counters when he can't afford toiletries. I can picture him, with remnants of once-palpable charm, winking his blue eyes as the blushing shop girl hands over the sample bottle of spray cologne.

After each cycle of mania, depression, and treatment, and with the help of our parents or public assistance, Milo has started life over and over again, with second-hand clothes, a used car, and a new job.

All goes well until he goes off his medications. "When I begin to get manic," he says, "I feel more energy and confidence. I don't want to spoil it by taking my pills."

At this point he often gets a second job. With little need for sleep, he can pour concrete during the day and deliver pizza at night. During this stage of mania, he might spend his few off hours riding a bicycle thirty miles from Reno, where he lives, on the busy highway to Carson City, or even still farther south to Genoa or Minden. And he writes mountains of letters to the editors of newspapers about some issue that has taken hold of his mind.

One day he cashes his paycheck and takes off for parts unknown, sometimes in his car, sometimes by bus. If he has enough money, he buys a one-way airline ticket from Reno to one of his favorite destinations, Las Vegas or Miami.

Days later, broke and hungry, he calls home in a deep depression. Someone in the family wires money and provides a plane or bus ticket back to Reno. He repays this debt by faithfully resuming his medications. That is, until he misses the euphoric high of mania and "doesn't need them anymore." Here, the cycle begins again.

Milo has been homeless many times, but never in trouble with the law until recently, when he finally crossed that line. Today, he is a convicted felon, with a legacy that will stay with him for the rest of his life.

Bipolar disorder affects people of all types and personalities. During manic and depressive episodes the disease may alter feelings and actions, but the core of one's basic character remains essentially the same. However, even at his best, when he is stabilized on medication, my brother seems to be no more mature than he was at age eighteen, when he first became sick. It is as if this illness has somehow arrested him in time.

Studies have shown the teenage brain to be long on charm and short on judgment, impulse control, and the ability to plan ahead. Milo's problems begin with decisions he makes with his "teenage brain" under the influence of mania. Even in the so-called "normal" phases of his life, he usually makes unfortunate choices.

There have been many studies and theories concerning bipolar disorder. However, in the mid-twentieth century, it was Marie-Louise von Franz, a Jungian psychologist, who introduced a certain personality type—not necessarily pathological in itself, called the *puer aeternus*, or "eternal boy." She developed a profile of character traits which seems to describe my brother. Add manic-depression to the mix, with its potential for delusions and hallucinations, and the eternal boy can have, and cause, eternal problems.

Von Franz says: "In general, the man who is identified with the archetype of the *puer aeternus* remains too long in adolescent psychology; that is, all those characteristics that are normal in a youth of seventeen or eighteen are continued …Generally the youthful charm of the *puer aeternus* is prolonged through later stages of life …"

This quality of youth contributes to Milo's ability to be charismatic, physically brave and venturesome. To this day he retains his wonderful sense of humor.

Von Franz goes on to say, "The one thing dreaded throughout by such a type of man is to be bound to anything whatever. There is a terrific fear of being pinned down …There is always the fear of being caught in a situation from which it may be impossible to slip out again. Every just-so situation is hell."

That's my brother!

Throughout his adult life, Milo has never been committed to one situation for long. Although this is mostly due to his illness, his actions reflect a chronic aversion to responsibility. When the net tightens, he literally escapes.

I find other startling parallels in the Von Franz profile: "With this there is often, to a smaller or greater extent, a savior complex, or a Messiah complex, with the secret thought that one day one will be able to save the world."

Before his adventures in Florida and subsequent trip to Cuba, my brother spent almost a decade on a one-man crusade to close the brothels in Nevada. He pulled many publicity stunts in order to promote this cause.

Von Franz uses the author of *The Little Prince*, Antoine de Saint-Exupéry, as an example of the *puer aeternus*. He spent much of his life as an aviator and died in a plane crash in World War II. She says that this type of person "never quite commits himself to any mundane situation but just hovers over the earth, touching it from time to time …"

From the time he was very small, Milo had a fascination with airplanes and was determined to learn to fly. When he was in his late teens, Milo took a few lessons from our father, a test pilot and flight instructor. From then on he was hooked.

In the story of *Peter Pan*, J. M. Barrie paints a graphic portrayal of the "eternal boy." Peter's Neverland includes only that which is fun and adventurous, not the mundane minutia involved in the difficult steps of growing up: "Neverland is always more or less an island, with astonishing splashes of colour here and there, and coral reefs and rakish-looking craft in the offing, and savages and lonely lairs, and gnomes who are mostly tailors, and caves through which a river runs … It would be an easy map if that were all; but there is also first day at school, religion, fathers, verbs … three-pence for pulling out your tooth yourself, and so on … and it is all rather confusing especially as nothing will stand still."

Barrie also gets it right when it comes to the charming but undependable qualities of this type of man-boy: "'Second to the right, and straight on till morning.' That, Peter had told Wendy, was the way to the Neverland; but even birds, carrying maps and consulting them at windy corners, could not have sighted it with these instructions. Peter, you see, just said anything that came into his head."

Adventure is the highest priority with the *puer aeternus* and Peter Pan. It comes before friends, family, and community ties: "Peter was not with them for the moment, and they felt rather lonely up there by themselves.

"He could go so much faster than they that he would suddenly shoot out of sight, to have some adventure in which they had no share. He would come down laughing over something fearfully funny he had been saying to a star, but he had already forgotten what it was ..."

When the adventure is over, Peter, like Milo, can count on his charm to assure that he is cared for and his needs are met: "He often went out alone, and when he came back you were never absolutely certain whether he had had an adventure or not. He might have forgotten it so completely that he said nothing about it ... Sometimes he came home with his head bandaged, and then Wendy cooed over him and bathed it in lukewarm water, while he told a dazzling tale." (1)

Bipolar disorder is an illness with a genetic link. Milo's son is also bipolar. Our father has had episodes of manic behavior, although he has never been officially diagnosed and treated. Siblings of victims often suffer from *unipolar* depression (episodes of depression without the mania).

An artist and teacher, I am able to relate to the thrill of being on a creative roll, which sometimes can be an almost manic feeling. I have also known the down side of that feeling, a state in which there is no earthly reason for anything at all. Depression always lurks a few steps behind. Sometimes it creeps up and threatens to attack, and I am grateful for medication that keeps it at bay.

However, manic-depressive illness can be another story. When serious, as in my brother's case, it is all-encompassing. At its worst, it is manifested in psychotic behavior. In many cases a person lives a sub-normal existence in which the original potential of the person is lost in a life of misjudgments and dysfunctional relationships.

In recent years great strides have been made in bipolar medications in combination with psychotherapy, and new treatments are in the experimental stages. However, there are still serious gaps in social services for people with mental illnesses of all kinds. The policy of deinstitutionalization in the 1970s and 1980s, in which many mental institutions were emptied, did not offer adequate alternatives for patients. Consequently, our jails and prisons took on the role of those former mental facilities.

Is there some kind of line between pathology and character? At what point is a person with mental illness accountable for his or her actions? Surely that person must take on some responsibility, especially when it comes to complying with medical orders. When this does not happen, should society step in?

With each recurring bout of this illness, Milo has caused damage to his life and to the lives of others. I am frustrated that there is no way to ensure that mentally ill people have access to appropriate treatment, and I feel despair at the fact that there is no way to ensure that people like my brother will *comply* with this treatment. In a democratic society this is a thorny problem. Where is that point at which the civil liberties of the mentally ill and the security of others are in balance?

I can only hope that Milo's story will shed a bit of light on this issue.

(1) Reprinted with the permission of Atheneum Books for Young Readers, an imprint of Simon & Schuster Children's Publishing Division, from *Peter Pan* by J. M. Barrie. Copyright 1911, Charles Scribner's Sons; Copyright 1939, Lady Cynthia Asquith and Peter Llewlyn Davies.

~~~

Undue emphasis has been placed on the "right" of seriously mentally ill individuals to refuse unwanted treatment. A better approach would balance this right against the rights of the public, who may be exposed to harm from untreated seriously mentally ill individuals. Seriously mentally ill individuals whom the courts deem potentially dangerous should be maintained on medication as a condition of living in the community.

– *Criminalizing the Seriously Mentally Ill: The Abuse of Jails as Mental Hospitals*, by Torrey, Stieber, Ezediel, Wolfe, Sharfstein, Noble, Flynn, a joint report of the National Alliance for the Mentally Ill and Public Citizen's Health Research Group, 1992

Part One:

Witness to Madness

It is the very error of the moon;
She comes more near the earth than she was wont
And makes men mad.

– William Shakespeare, *Othello*, V, ii

There is a particular kind of pain, elation, loneliness, and terror involved in this kind of madness. When you're high it's tremendous. The ideas and feelings are fast and frequent like shooting stars, and you follow them until you find better and brighter ones ... But somewhere this changes.
   An Unquiet Mind, Kay Redfield Jamison, Alfred A. Knopf, Inc., New York, 1995

Chapter One: On a Cuban Beach

July 31, 2001

Rolando Gonzales made his way up the rocky coast. Summer was the hurricane season, but today the sky was clear. A thunderstorm might come in by tomorrow.

He had been lucky this morning. Three fish, caught in the surf with his new pole. Someday he hoped to buy a boat, go out into deeper waters and catch enough to sell in the marketplace in his village of Cojímar. Perhaps then he could earn enough to fix the car, an inheritance from his uncle, a 1956 Buick. He had a friend who could get parts for it, but they were expensive. His cousin José kept a 1957 Chevrolet running by improvising with old tractor parts. But Rolando was afraid to ask him for help because he already owed him money. Besides, even if the Buick was in running condition, how could he afford to buy gasoline?

Rolando had heard about people who built boats or rafts and tried to make it to Florida. Some were sent back; some drowned. He was not ready for that.

He stopped to listen. The soft lapping of the waves was being drowned out by the growing sound of an engine. Rolando looked up and saw a small plane approaching in a downward glide towards the shore. It made a turn, and the engine sputtered as it seemed to dance over the water. One of its wheels hit a large rock, and it flipped upside down, skidding down the beach, leaving clouds of sand.

Rolando ran toward the plane. Its tires were still spinning. The door crept open, upward, against gravity. A tall, light-haired man worked his way out of the cockpit, climbed down to the beach, looked around, then lurched backward and dropped to his knees. His head was bleeding, but he seemed not to notice. The man's blue eyes looked through and past Rolando; he did not respond when asked, *"Cómo está usted, señor?"*

By the writing on its side and the numbers on the wing, Rolando could see that the plane was from the U.S.A. He had heard some military jets in the sky earlier and then seen them bank into a wide circle and disappear. That was not unusual. Although American planes were not officially permitted in Cuban airspace, they often came close to shore. But Rolando had never seen a foreign plane actually land on Cuban soil.

Other people began to arrive. Rolando told them what he had seen. Someone tried to communicate with the man in English, but he did not respond. When the police arrived an hour later, he still sat with a wide-eyed, unfocused gaze.

The police asked the man his name. He turned to look at them for the first time, then, in English, he said, "My name is Juan Miguel. I've come to save your country."

An hour before, Milo had been taking his final flying lesson at Paradise Aviation in the Florida Keys by soloing in a Cessna 172. According to Milo, the crash landing in Cuba was not the only close call during his renegade flight from Marathon Airport that day:

After making three take-offs and landings with him, my instructor told me to take off alone and make one trip around the field and land. When the plane was in the air, I reported to Marathon Unicom that I was in distress. I then flew toward Key West and due south toward the island [of Cuba].

An hour later, I spotted an air force recon plane circling. On its third pass it flew close, and the wake turbulence from its engines put my plane into a dive. I let go of the yoke and rudder, as I had read in the textbook, and the plane righted itself.

Finally, I saw the whitecaps of the ocean turn to one long white line. These were waves approaching the shore and I realized I had reached Cuba. At that time, all I could think of was landing. I was afraid of being shot at like the "Brothers to the Rescue."

I noticed what looked like a road and slowed the plane as much as I could with full flaps. I landed on some rocks and the plane nosed over.

~~~

When once again a bottle of medication is found in the trash bin, when we are told to mind our own business, that we are the only one who has a problem, when yet another doctor's appointment is missed, we all come one step closer to throwing our hands up in despair. Sometimes, whether or not we walk away, our loved ones do. They disappear for hours, days, weeks and even years. Some reach the headlines.
– *I Am Not Sick I Don't Need Help*, Xavier Amador, Ph.D., Vida Press, 2000, p.11

Bipolar disorder, also called manic-depressive illness, is a serious disorder of the brain. More than 2.3 million American adults, or about one percent of the population in a given year, have bipolar disorder. Abnormalities in brain biochemistry and in the structure and/or activity of certain brain circuits are responsible for the extreme shifts in mood, energy, and functioning that characterize bipolar disorder.
    – National Institute of Mental Health, http://www.nimh.nih.gov

Chapter Two: The Nightly News

Reno, Nevada, August 9, 2001

Ted and I had driven almost four hundred miles that day, after a week-long vacation in Oregon. Thunder vibrated over the mountains outside Reno to the north. The local radio station reported several fires started by lightning, and we could hear the drone of air tankers overhead.

"God, my back hurts," Ted said as we drove into the Super 8 Motel.

We unloaded the car. I made a mental note to call Dad and tell him that we were here. Although it was almost seven in the evening, the thermometer outside the motel office read ninety-four degrees. Santa Barbara had spoiled us with its fog-cooled summers.

Ted collapsed on the bed and turned on the television news. I started unpacking. "What do you want to do for dinner?" I asked. "How about we just send out for pizza? I'm exhausted. By the way, can you turn that down a bit?"

"Here is the news for Thursday, August ninth ..."

"Pizza? With all these great restaurants? In all these great casinos?" Ted's eyes twinkled as he shook the container of quarters he had been filling up for weeks.

"If we call Domino's, maybe Milo will make the delivery," I mused as I took a swig of Diet Coke. "Isn't that where he's working now? Or is it Rusty's?"

It was then that I heard the announcer say, "The ex-Reno man who crashed his plane a week ago on a rocky beach in Cuba is back on U.S. soil tonight. Cuban officials flew him to Miami today, where the F.B.I. took him into custody. Milo John Reese ..."

"Turn it up!"

I stared at the T.V., twisting and untwisting the tank top I had just peeled off. Ted pointed the remote at the screen. Just then, we watched my brother Milo limp down the steps of a plane, his hands cuffed together. A woman in uniform escorted him away.

"...faces fifteen years for transporting stolen property."

"Holy shit!" Ted heaved himself off his bed.

"He crashed a plane? A week ago?" I groped for the nearest chair.

We had not watched TV or seen a newspaper for the past week.

"Remember what Dad said on the phone last week?" I reminded. "That Milo was talking about taking one of his trips? And not taking his pills? And acting sick again?"

"Sure." Ted nodded his head slowly. "But how did he get to *Cuba*?"

I put my sweaty tank top back on and went next door to the 7-Eleven. There was one issue of the *Reno Gazette-Journal* left on the newsstand. On the front page, there was a photo of Milo in handcuffs, an agonized expression on his face. The article described a novice pilot who had flown from the Florida Keys to Cuba on his solo flight. As I walked back to our room, the sky was a surreal red. I could smell the smoke from the fires now.

At 5:30 the next morning, I stood by the open curtain to watch the aspen trees in the park across the street begin to take shape. Though I had barely slept, I decided to go for a walk while it was still cool.

As I adjusted my earphones, a local radio announcer recited the contest question of the day: "Why did Milo John Reese say he was treated like a king by the Cuban government after he crash-landed near Havana?"

The winning answer: "Because he's a royal PAIN!"

Milo seemed to be a well-known figure around here. But after a decade of antics to call attention to a campaign against the brothels, I guessed that Nevada had had enough of him.

Ever since I can remember, I've had a recurring dream. I'm in the middle of a field watching a single engine yellow plane in the sky overhead. The engine begins to sputter. The aircraft heads my way and dives nose first into the ground next to me. I stand there waiting for it to explode.

During the days after Milo made headlines, this dream haunted me again. I tried to feel grateful that he had not been killed in the plane crash. I thought about this six weeks later, as we watched the images of 9-11, saw the faces of the nineteen hijackers, and learned that some of them, too, were taking flying lessons in Florida during that summer.

We got on the Internet. After typing in "Milo John Reese," we found that there were over two hundred articles about him in news media all over the world, from Toledo to Thailand.

I wanted to scream at Milo, "How could you do such a thing? How could you just abandon your family on yet another wild mission sparked by some demon in your head? What about Kevin? Now everyone will know he's the son of that crazy nut who flew to Cuba! Don't you know what you've put Dad through? Don't you care?"

Before Milo was diagnosed with a severe mental disorder, in his late teens, our middle-class family had never known anyone who was bankrupt, homeless, or convicted of a serious crime. Now, during the course of his manic-depressive illness over the last forty years, Milo had exposed us to all these. I reminded myself that Milo was sick, that screaming would not change things. My brain understood this; my gut was still angry. In the weeks to come, I would wake up many nights, and the impact of the event would sock me in the stomach.

Why was I reacting this way? There was also a feeling of *déjà vu,* and a little-child fear that something scary was happening again. I realized now that flying away in a plane was a reenactment of the times our father had done exactly that when we were small.

~~~

Chronicity: SMI [severe mental illness] grief is also in a special category because it wells up in response to an ongoing illness. Chronic conditions entail chronic grief, rather than sudden or anticipatory grief. To think in terms of anticipating death or loss while the person with SMI still lives is to run the risk of feeling guilty about abandoning him or her. On the other hand, something surely has been lost. It is a complex situation for families to experience and sort out.

– *The Skipping Stone: Ripple Effects of Mental Illness on the Family by* Mona Wasow, Clinical Professor, Science & Behavior Books, Inc., Palo Alto, CA, 1995, pp. 103-104

Part Two:

The California Dream

*He rode upon a cherub, and did fly:
yea, he did fly upon the wings of the wind.*

– Psalms 18: 10

Today, many people feel that ADHD [Attention Deficit Hyperactivity Disorder] has become a fad diagnosis ... However, when today's adults with bipolar disorders were children, ADHD was not recognized as often, and childhood-onset bipolar disorders were usually missed altogether.
    – *Adult Bipolar Disorders: Understanding Your Diagnosis & Getting Help,* by Mitzi Waltz, O'Reilly Media, Inc., 2002

Chapter Three: San Fernando Valley, 1945-1950

    Three days before my brother was born, on November 24, 1945, my father's best friend, Milo Burcham, a fellow test pilot for Lockheed Aviation, was demonstrating the company's first jet airplane. After taking off, Burcham flew fast and low in front of a group of executives lined up beside the runway. Suddenly, the engine quit. The pilot tried to ease up the plane, but it hit a sandpit at the end of the runway and went in on its belly. Milo Burcham was killed instantly. My brother became his namesake. Throughout his childhood, my brother would ask Dad to tell stories about him.
    I was the eldest child; my sister, Carolyn, was born three years later. Milo came two years after that. We spent our childhood in the San Fernando Valley when it was a rural paradise of alfalfa fields, walnut orchards, and ranches owned by familiar movie names like Jack Warner, Robert Taylor, and Barbara Stanwyck.

Our maternal grandparents had come out from New York in the late 1930s. Boppop, as we called him, was retired from his position as a bank vice president in New York and intended to become a gentleman farmer. He and Nana purchased twenty-five acres, built a large, two-story, California-style farmhouse, a stable, and two barns. They fenced a large pasture in which to raise thoroughbred horses. Our parents built a house next door, and it was here that we three children spent much of our childhood.

Every summer, Boppop planted football field-sized patches of corn, tomatoes, and squash. The rest of the land was leased to local farmers. The monotony of alfalfa was sometimes broken by other crops, and one year it was watermelons. When the workers left, we joined other neighborhood kids to traipse into the fields carrying knives and saltshakers. I can still picture Milo with watermelon juice running down his delighted face, staining the little shirt Mom had just ironed.

On those mornings when we heard the sound of the crop duster's bi-plane, we children, still wearing our pajamas with the built-in feet and flaps on the butt, would run out to the end of the neatly planted rows that backed up to our house. Jumping up and down, we yelled to the pilot, daring him with our bodies not to pull up until the very last second. The plane would tilt his wings back and forth as if waving to us, but it was gone all too soon, on to the next field, leaving us unaware of the deadly dust of DDT drifting toward us.

After World War II, when small planes were no longer grounded, my father bought a narrow piece of land at the back of my grandfather's property on which he created an airstrip runway and built a small hangar for his Piper Cub airplane. Here, he gave private flying lessons to supplement his income as a test pilot.

It was a treat to take a ride in my father's plane. Milo followed Dad around constantly, and, from the time he was big enough to wear a seatbelt, he took many flights with him in the back seat of the Piper Cub. I remember Dad waving to us on the ground as they took off on the dirt runway, Milo's blond head barely visible behind him. At three years old, Milo decided that he was going to be a pilot when he grew up, and his collection of toy planes expanded each Christmas.

Milo's bed looked like an airfield, with bombers lined up beside fighter planes, ready to take off. I can still see him holding a small P-51 and "flying" it through the air as he uttered "*Vroom, Vroom, Vroom!*"

Recently, Milo related this childhood memory:

I am three years old. I wake up early and look out the window. The fog is thick, an outside porch light just visible. My father's landing strip is across the field. At one end, there is a small hangar, and inside it, a brand new, bright yellow Piper Cub airplane. I've walked hand in hand many times with my Dad to the little airport to fly the Cub. This morning I will walk there alone. This time, I will fly alone.

I feel very brave. I put my shoes on, grab my Teddy, "Norford," push the window open, jump through, and fall to the ground. I slip out through the back gate and trudge through the field. Except for a hint of sunrise, the morning is dark and still. The stubble, rocks, and dirt clods don't stop me. The alfalfa is half as tall as I am, and it's wet. I'm drenched, but I push on toward the sunrise. I have to fly the Cub before my Dad wakes up. This adventure has to be a secret. Just me, the Cub, and Norford will ever know.

There it is, finally. The hangar. Inside, the Cub. A big airplane toy, not much different from the toy planes in my bedroom. I jump into the front seat and toss Norford in the back. The hangar has no doors. I turn the propeller, start the engine, and take off. My Daddy always makes it look so easy.

I fly the plane into the clouds, higher and higher, then upside down, doing loops. I fly beside passenger planes and helicopters and blimps. Then I fly close to the ground, so close I can touch it. I fly right into a storm. The Cub shakes violently, and I'm shaking, too. I open my eyes, and Dad is shaking me awake.

We lived on Shoup Avenue, a main thoroughfare for traffic from Ventura Boulevard into Canoga Park. Many of our cats were lost to the slaughter of the cars, and our parents were strict about keeping us well away from the street. During World War II a battalion of army tanks had come along, and the asphalt was forever scarred with their metal tread marks. In post-war years, with a growing economy, more trucks appeared, along with shiny, faster new cars.

One morning, when I was in third grade and Carolyn in kindergarten, Mom was driving us to school in Nana's old Buick sedan. I rode in the front seat, my sister and three-year-old Milo in back. I turned in my seat as I heard a sudden rush of air and the sound of squealing brakes. Carolyn was leaning out the door, screaming. By that time Mom had the car stopped. She was running toward Milo, who lay face down on the street. There was a huge truck parked behind us.

Mom sank to her knees and carefully cradled Milo's head in her lap. It reminded me of the Nativity scene we got out every Christmas, with a glass figurine of Mary holding the baby Jesus. But there was blood everywhere, all over Milo's head, his clothes, now on Mom's skirt.

"Lady, it was sheer luck that I saw him fall out of the car," the truck driver muttered as he climbed down from the cab. "One more second, I couldn't have stopped this rig."

It was a long moment before the fierce, reassuring wail began.

"If there's pain, there's feeling, Ma'am. A good sign."

Another passing driver stopped. He ran to the nearest house to phone for an ambulance. Carolyn and I now stood behind Mom.

"What happened?" Mom turned to Carolyn. "I told you to watch him!"

"He just leaned over and opened the door." Carolyn's cheeks were streaked with guilty tears. "I reached for him and he just went out!"

Milo had quieted down now, and we heard the faint sound of a siren.

There is a family photograph of my brother with his head in a large bandage. In his hand is a toy airplane.

Sixteen years later, in the early 1960s, when Milo was diagnosed with mental illness, my father asked the psychiatrist if his boyhood accident might have been a factor. The doctor was doubtful, but he admitted that medical science just hadn't come far enough to answer that question precisely.

~~~

Occasional cases of head injury causing severe depression or mania have been reported in the psychiatric literature for almost one hundred years ... Indeed, for both depression and mania, it is difficult to assess whether the head injury was directly causal, how much time could have elapsed between the injury and the psychiatric symptoms, and whether the head injury merely precipitated a reaction that was about to occur, even if the injury had not taken place ... It appears that head injuries can at least occasionally either cause or precipitate episodes of mania and the full syndrome of manic-depressive illness.
– *Surviving Manic Depression* by E. Fuller Torrey, M.D. & Michael B. Knable, D.O., Basic Books, 2002, p. 72-73

A lack of impulse control is...demonstrated by the extreme hyperactivity of children and adolescents with bipolar illness. Whereas the average child may have periods of great physical energy, the child...with bipolar disorder has periods of energy that are out of control and lacking in structure and direction.
– *New Hope for People with Bipolar Disorder*, by Jan Fawcett, M.D., Bernard Golden, Ph.D., Nancy Rosenfeld, copyright 2000 by Jan Fawcett, Bernard Golden, and Nancy Rosenfeld. Used by permission of Prima Publishing, a division of Random House, Inc.

Chapter Four: Growing Up, 1950-1960

To this day, the sound of a small plane sends a signal to the part of my brain that is still ten years old. That sound meant Dad was coming home. He would buzz the house before he landed on his airstrip nearby. He might be away on business. But he might be returning from one of those mysterious other trips which he sometimes took once or twice a year.

After each trip, Dad would return smiling, bringing us rare presents—perfume for Mom, tiny candy balls inside a miniature orange crate for me, Hallmark dolls for Carolyn, a toy airplane for Milo. I have thought about these trips many times in the past few years and wondered at their significance in view of what later happened.

* * *

When our parents met, in 1938, Dad was twenty-one, Mom barely eighteen. Mom was coming down the stairs of a library when she locked eyes with a handsome, dark-haired man. She claimed to know at that moment that she would marry him. After two months, they eloped in the brand new Ford V-8 that her father had bought her after she had given up candy for a year.

It was only a short walk to our grandparents' house, where I spent many hours improvising simple songs on Nana's baby grand piano and helping Boppop irrigate his vegetable garden. We children would play school in the front library; I was the teacher, Carolyn and Milo my disobedient students. We would be likely to get in trouble when the three of us were together, rolling cigarettes out of dried walnut leaves in the orchard, or digging a swimming hole in the front lawn.

Our grandparents were frustrated with Milo's whirlwind behavior. Like a puppy wagging its tail, Milo would throw his arms this way and that as he came perilously close to Nana's antiques. "Maarlo," Boppop would say, in a Pennsylvania pronunciation of Milo's name. "You can't fly your plane in here."

Nana would put her hands on her hips and sigh.

When Milo was five or six, I remember times when he would wake up screaming. Once, I went into his bedroom to see Mom trying to comfort him.

"It was just a nightmare," Mom cooed as she rocked him back and forth.

"But Jesus was trying to kill me," he whined over and over.

As he got older, Milo's awkwardness diminished, and he became a favorite choice in playground games. He seemed fearless, and his athletic skills improved. His childhood became typical of a boy growing up in the 1950s, with Little League, Cub Scouts, Sheriff John Birthday parties, a red Schwinn bicycle, and afternoon fishing trips with his friends to the wash at the edge of the field behind our house.

When Milo was thirteen, Dad sold the airstrip, and our parents bought a new, custom home at the west end of the Valley. During the nineteen fifties, suburbia had crept steadily outward from Los Angeles, and the once-green fields sprouted tract houses. Shopping centers replaced former orchards. Smog began to creep over the Hollywood Hills. I went away to college.

Milo and Dad started building a water skiing boat, and the family garage was converted to a workshop. After months of sawing, sanding, shaping, and painting, the boat was ready for an outboard motor and its launch into a nearby lake. Only Milo seemed to be able to get up, and stay up, on skis behind this underpowered vessel. He quickly became an able skier, doing tricks such as raising one ski straight up as he bounced over the small waves. Hanging on to the rope with one hand, he would wave to us on the shore as he passed by.

It was during this time that Dad began calling Milo "Friend of All Friends," an apt description. Teachers at school reported his popularity with other students. They remarked on his amazing ability to settle disputes with other boys. In junior high school, Milo was elected student body president and presented with trophies for "Best Scholar" and "Best Athlete."

Two years later, in high school, Milo was the star quarterback on the football team. After one triumphant game, Carolyn and two friends ran out on the field to congratulate him for making a touchdown. He was surrounded by a circle of female fans.

During one football season, it was discovered that Milo had played two games with a broken foot, and when my parents asked him why he hadn't said something about the pain, he answered, "I couldn't let the team down."

But there were some odd things about Milo even then. Once, Ted and I watched from the stands as the football players did warm-up exercises. A hundred blue and white jersey arms and legs were in sync, except for one lone figure off to the side. Milo jumped when the others jacked, and he stared off toward the end zone, seeming to hear a rhythm inside his head entirely his own.

One afternoon, in the spring of his sophomore year, Milo said he was going to see his friend Jeff down the street. At nine that night, when he still had not come home, Mom called Jeff's parents. They had not seen Milo. Dad spent hours driving around, looking for him.

At two in the morning, just as Mom was about to call the police, Milo returned, his red eyes open wide. He had no explanation for his behavior.

That next fall, during a parent night at school, the football coach leaned towards Dad's ear. "There's something wrong with Milo's brain," he whispered.

Dad was puzzled. Later, the meaning of this statement would become clear.

~~~

Mood and energy swings often precede overt clinical illness by years (about one-third of patients with definite manic-depressive illness, for example, report bipolar mood swings...predating the actual onset of their illness). These typically begin in adolescence or early adulthood and occur most often in the spring or autumn.
– *Touched with Fire: Manic-Depressive Illness and the Artistic Temperament*, by Kay Redfield Jamison, Free Press, a division of Simon & Schuster, Inc., 1993

There is clear evidence that in the period leading up to first becoming ill, people will often have experienced significant changes or problems in their lives. The level of these [changes] will usually be higher than those experienced by people who do not become ill.
 – *Coping with Bipolar Disorder: A Guide to Living with Manic-Depression*, by Steven Jones, Peter Hayward, & Dominic Lam, Oneworld, Oxford, 2002

Chapter Five: The Storm

June 1961

For several years our parents made trips all over the west in searching for a cattle ranch. Perhaps it was the stress of the ever-encroaching suburban landscape, or maybe my father's urge to escape a job he disliked.

Looking back, I wonder if this quest might have contained an urge to save their marriage, along with Dad's sanity. Although they knew nothing about raising cattle and alfalfa, Mom took agriculture courses at a nearby community college; Dad subscribed to the *Farm Journal*.

Gradually, after they saved enough money for a down payment, realtors in rural areas from Arizona to Montana became familiar with Oscar and Charlotte Reese as they took them over rutted and muddy roads to show them ranch after ranch.

One day soon after my wedding, Mom called me in Santa Barbara to tell me that they had found "the place." The Callahan

Ranch, as it was called, was located in central Nevada off Highway 50, twenty-five miles from the town of Austin. I'd heard of Austin, Texas, but never Austin, Nevada. Not many other people had heard of it either, since it had a population of only seventy-five.

That April, Mom had gone ahead of the rest of the family to live at the ranch with Addie Callahan, the former owner, while she was still there. Mom thought it was important to learn all she could about running the place, and she took careful notes on such things as when to brand, when to bring the cows in for the winter, and which buyers paid the best prices.

Dad, Carolyn, and Milo stayed in Woodland Hills until the school year was over, and Dad could finally quit his job for good.

Sometimes Mom got through to us on the phone, when the lines were not down due to storms. When she did call, we had to watch what we said, since there were seven other ranches on the line.

"I feel like I've taken a time machine back into the nineteenth century," she laughed. "Like we saw on that one episode of *The Twilight Zone*."

With the exception of two tractors, a bailer, and a 1948 Jeep pickup, the Callahan was mostly as it had been for one hundred years. The cows were rounded up by horseback and branded by the old methods of roping and tying. There were two plow horses to be harnessed when the old John Deere broke down.

With no electricity, cooking had to be done on an ancient wood stove. Potatoes stayed cool in the underground cellar on the side of the hill out back. Mom filled the teakettle and washed clothes in the stream that ran by the kitchen door. She was grateful for the "insider" bathroom which had been the one recent addition to the house.

It was mid-June, the last day of school. The house in Woodland Hills had finally sold, and Carolyn, who had been put in charge of keeping the house neat and clean, was relieved of the pressure to keep it looking like *House and Garden*.

Today had been a short schedule at Canoga Park High; Carolyn and Milo arrived home by noon. They now sat in front of the TV watching a Roy Rogers movie and celebrating summer with bowls of chocolate mint ice cream and Girl Scout peanut butter cookies.

Dad had told them that they should start packing. But escrow on the house would take another ten days, and Carolyn figured that she would have plenty of time to go to the beach, say goodbye to her friends, and see a few movies before she attacked her room and cleaned the house one final time.

When the phone rang, it was the usual sibling dialogue.

"You get it."

"No, you get it."

"I got it last time."

"No you didn't."

"Yes, I did ..."

Carolyn finally picked up the receiver on the fifth ring. "Carolyn? This is Dad. Can you and Milo be packed in an hour?"

"For what?"

"To move to Nevada. That's what. Bring one suitcase each. I borrowed the company plane. Put the cats in boxes and round up Muldoon."

"Egad!"

"I'll see you in a little while. Bye."

"But Dad ..."

He had hung up. *We shouldn't be surprised*, thought Carolyn. *Dad always does things this way.*

They plopped their dirty bowls in the sink and did a mad scramble to cram as much as they could into some old pieces of luggage. Carolyn swept everything off the top of her dresser into her Starlite makeup case. (Dad would just *have* to let her bring this!)

As Milo stuffed his favorite issues of *Mad Magazine* into his bursting duffle bag, they heard Dad's car. "You guys ready?" he called.

"Dad, I can't find Tobey."

They finally found the cat in the dirty clothes basket in the bathroom, the same basket where she had given birth to her last batch of kittens. Milo shoved her in one of the boxes he had prepared with breathing holes cut out with a kitchen knife.

Inside was an old cake pan full of sand from the back yard. Tobey began a constant litany of yowls.

Carolyn looked around; the house was a mess. But Dad would be back one last time to load the furniture into a van.

"Let him worry about it," she muttered.

An hour later, the three of them were piling luggage and animals into a twin-engine Piper Aztec airplane at the Van Nuys airport. Oscar had promised to have the plane back by sundown the next day. This explained the short notice.

As he taxied the plane to the end of the runway, Oscar said, "Make sure you keep your seat belts on the whole time, kids. It can get bumpy over the mountains."

"What was that noise?" Carolyn was the one member of the family who did not enjoy flying. She sat gripping her seat.

"Don't worry," Milo answered. "It's just Tobey trying to get out of her box." On cue, there was a loud meow accompanied by scratching sounds. A minute later, just as he was about to press full throttle for take-off, Oscar had a hissing cat climbing all over the controls.

"Carolyn, come get this animal! I told you guys to box them up well!"

"But you also told us to keep our seat belts on ..."

"Now!" Oscar yelled.

Meanwhile, the ten-month old German shepherd Muldoon slept through everything, splayed out on his own seat, drugged just before they left home with a pain killer from the medicine cabinet.

"Other Cat's getting out of her box, too!" Carolyn retrieved Tobey as Milo dived for Other Cat, just missing a connection of his hands around the black and white torso as the creature streaked around the cabin.

Forty-five minutes into the trip, the plane was on a steady north-east course. The cats emitted only an occasional meow from their boxes. There was still no movement from Muldoon.

The Sierras appeared to the left, their tops whipped cream white even though it was early summer. Milo looked down at the landscape below. Dad seemed to be following the silver ribbon of a road which ran straight up the valley.

Soon, Milo noticed a few tiny buildings, like monopoly tokens, dotting the fields, then clusters of these as the plane approached what appeared to be a town. As they flew over the north end, the highway forked, one part veering left toward the mountains to the west. Dad continued northeast, above the road that led toward another mountain range.

"There's Montgomery Pass," Oscar pointed out. "We just left the town of Bishop, and we'll be crossing over the Nevada border in a minute."

Carolyn was just beginning to relax when they felt the first bumps of turbulence. Dark clouds began to wrap themselves around the aircraft; saucer-sized raindrops spattered the cockpit windshield. Oscar switched on the cabin lights as the storm assaulted the fuselage. Soon the rain turned to snow. Milo grinned through the window with excitement. Carolyn, white-faced, sat stiff in her seat, eyes closed.

They were over what Oscar called Smokey Valley. The turbulence subsided a bit, but now the rain came again, assaulting them in sheets.

"I'm going to try and set her down if I can find a place. We'll wait out this weather and then go on ..." Oscar's voice sounded less confident than his words.

"Hey, Dad," Milo called, "I think I see a runway!"

Oscar banked the plane. Sure enough, there was a small airstrip down there, and there was even a wind sock which signaled the direction to land.

When the plane was almost on the ground, it was buffeted by a sudden gust of wind. Oscar fought to keep the controls steady, then touched down on the rutted muddy surface. They bounced along, sliding and slipping from side to side. Finally the aircraft came to a stop.

All was quiet for several moments. Muldoon gave a yelp, and Carolyn and Milo started clapping. "Ya did good, Dad!" they chimed.

Now what? The Callahan ranch was still fifty miles away, in another valley. Dad unfastened his seat belt, zipped up his jacket, and opened the cabin door. "I hear an engine," he said, as he tried to hold the door open in the wind. Just then, Muldoon jumped out, running off into the rain-blurred sagebrush.

A blue pickup truck was pulling up parallel to the right wing of the plane. A man wearing a slicker and a cowboy hat jumped out. They barely heard what he was yelling over the relentless din of the rain.

"You all can come to the house and wait this out, if you want!"

The three travelers sat by the fire in the rancher's living room, drinking cocoa and eating donuts. They had left the cats inside the plane, but their calls for Muldoon had yielded only scared jack rabbits.

"Ya know," said the rancher out of the side of his pipe, "doesn't look like this storm's lettin' up. You could take my other truck, if you like. Then bring it back when you return for your airplane."

"Are you sure?" Oscar's face lighted up. "Gee, that's nice of you."

When they returned to the Aztec, they piled the luggage and the boxed-up cats under a tarpaulin in the bed of the pickup. There was still no sign of relief in the storm. No sign of Muldoon, either.

Milo, Carolyn, and Oscar squeezed into the cab, and they began the slow journey to the main highway, windshield wipers working just fast enough to give a dim picture of the dirt road they were following.

At nine o'clock that same night, Charlotte was reading a paperback western by the light of an oil lamp at the old oak table in the dining room. She looked up and thought she saw something through the rain-streaked window. Lights were weaving their way through the poplar trees along the drive to the house. Who could *that* be? she wondered.

"Hi, Mom!" Milo called as he knocked. As she opened the door, she could see he was dripping wet, his hair slicked dark from rain. He came in holding a cardboard box and put it down beside the rocking chair. It emitted an oppressed "Meow."

"Good grief! How did you get here?"

Oscar came next, carrying another box, a tired smile on his face. Carolyn ran in behind him, gave Mom a hug, and said, "I'll never get on a plane again!"

Mom added wood to the stove in the kitchen and heated up three cans of Campbell's chicken-noodle soup. This she proudly served with her own homemade bread. "You've become a real pioneer woman, Char," Oscar said as he slurped and chewed.

"Shush, not too loud. Addie Callahan is asleep in there." Charlotte pointed down the hall. "If she were awake, you'd be eating mutton. That's practically all we've had every night since I've been here."

"Why not beef steaks, Mom? I thought this was a cattle ranch!" Milo was tipping the last of the soup into his mouth.

"Addie explained to me that you don't want to slaughter your capital. So we had to go to a sheep ranch and buy a lamb. If she'd had her way, it would have been an old ewe, but that's where I drew the line."

Charlotte suddenly got up from the table. "I just remembered the pie I made yesterday with the rest of the apples in the cellar. Addie picked them last fall off those two trees in the front yard."

They discussed what chores needed to be done until Oscar could return. They decided that Milo would help Herbie, the ranch hand, irrigate the lower meadow.

The cows had been let out on the open range for the summer, and they were starting to drop their calves. Herbie would teach Carolyn and Charlotte to ride the cow horses, so they could start bringing the calves in for branding.

"Egad," Carolyn said. "That sounds as dangerous as flying!"

Charlotte brought out the pie, her face beaming with pride. She carefully cut three large pieces, making a ritual of serving each person.

"I'm sorry there's no whipped cream," she apologized. "We haven't been to town for over a week."

Milo was the first to wince after taking a huge bite. Then Oscar puckered his mouth as he put down his fork. Carolyn made a gagging sound.

"What's the matter?" Charlotte looked at them. Then she grabbed a fork and tasted Oscar's pie. "I guess that tin in the pantry marked 'Sugar' was really *salt*," she said.

For years afterward, Charlotte was teased whenever she served pie for dessert, whatever the kind.

The next day dawned clear. The only evidence of the storm was some mud in the horse corral. Carolyn and Milo started exploring. They introduced themselves to Herbie, the ranch hand, who was drinking coffee and having a smoke out behind his log-walled bunkhouse. They petted Mac, the Australian cow dog, who followed them up the road by the stream which led through the main canyon of the ranch, its banks forested with aspen leaves dancing in the early summer sun. The hills were dotted with sagebrush and pinion pine. Meadow grass waved in the morning breeze. Up ahead was Mt. Callahan, over 10,000 feet high, tall enough to earn a place on the Nevada roadmap.

"What do you think of this place?" Carolyn asked as she picked a strange yellow wildflower.

"Just like the Ponderosa," Milo answered as he looked out down the valley. "Too bad it's so far from civilization."

When they got back to the house, Charlotte had pancake batter ready to pour on the griddle, and an elderly lady sat at the breakfast table with Oscar.

"Addie, this is Carolyn, and Milo," Mom gestured. "Kids, this is Miss Callahan."

The old lady turned her fierce brown eyes on them, a gaze which belied her otherwise frail appearance.

"Good flying weather," Oscar said, looking out at the brilliant sunlight. "I should be back in about a week. They told me the escrow papers on the house down there would be ready to sign on Friday. Then I'll rent a trailer and bring the rest of the stuff."

To Carolyn and Milo he said, "You guys help all you can, OK?"

"Don't forget my record player," Carolyn warned.

"But you can't play it here, remember?" Milo said. "No electric plugs!"

"Oh, I forgot. Well, bring it anyway. I'll take it to school with me in the fall. They do have electricity at the University of Nevada, don't they? Or is this whole state in a time warp?"

Oscar looked into his coffee cup as he said, "Too bad about Muldoon." The table was silent for a moment.

"Your dog was probably a nice dinner for a mountain lion," speculated Addie, as she raised a teacup to her lips. The family looked at her aghast.

An hour later, when Oscar drove up to the airplane, a shivering Muldoon waited for him under the wing. Oscar watched as the dog ate the peanut butter and jelly sandwich Char had made, as well as two hardboiled eggs.

~~~

Changes are a part of life, and sometimes they are quite welcome. Some of them are positive and some quite negative ... Manic and depressive episodes often follow major life changes, both positive and negative.

– *The Bipolar Disorder Survival Guide*, by David J. Miklowitz, PhD, The Guilford Press, New York/London, 2002, p. 90

Part Three:

The Wild West

*They change their skies above them,
But not their hearts that roam.*

– Rudyard Kipling, *The Nativeborn* (1895)

The diagnostic slipperiness of mania is abetted by the masks that it can adopt. One is that of "plausible sanity," where, under pressure of public scrutiny, self-control reasserts itself ... The result, unfortunately, is that many in the throes of mania have charmed their way out of the care they desperately need.
    – *A Mood Apart: The Thinker's Guide to Emotion and its Disorders,* Peter C. Whybrow, M.D., Harper-Perennial, a Division of HarperCollins Publishers, 1998, p. 58

Chapter Six: You Wanna Go to Elko?

July 1963

In the early 1960s, when my family owned the ranch, Ted and I spent summers there helping out during haying season. Working together, Ted and Milo formed a lifelong friendship. Over dinner each night, they would joke and tease each other while they told the rest of us about their adventures in the lower meadow. One day, they bailed a rattlesnake along with the hay. Another time, the bailer got stuck, and they proposed that the rest of us hands, Mom, Dad, Carolyn and I, would be called out to drive every ranch vehicle in a tethered line to pull it out.

That next morning, after nine or ten tries, the motley procession made up of two tractors, one pickup, a cattle truck, Carolyn's old Ford, and Ted's Kharman Ghia, was in sync.

Finally, the bailer rose out of the mud with a loud suck, spattering its goop on the surrounding windrows of alfalfa.

One summer, Mom asked Ted if he would take Milo to Elko for a dental appointment in mid-July. During the weeks before the trip, bucking bales of hay, Ted and Milo talked of little else.. They would feast on giant hamburgers and French fries washed down with Coca-Cola, scarce commodities at the ranch. Visit the Commercial Hotel to get a look at the world's largest stuffed polar bear. Take a swim in the motel pool. Ted would play the slots at the Stockman's Casino. Milo planned to spend his evening watching TV in the motel room, something he had not done on the ranch.

One late afternoon, three days before they left for Elko, Ted and Milo were given the chore of replacing the salt licks up on Mount Callahan. With Ted at the wheel, they lumbered up the main canyon over the seldom-used, rutted dirt road in the ancient four-wheel drive Jeep. With stops to open the two gates on the way, it took them an hour to climb the steep slope to the end of the road.

When the Jeep refused to go any farther, Ted set the brake. Milo shoved a large rock behind each of the rear wheels. Together, they carried ten fifty-pound blocks of salt up the last two hundred yards, one by one. The wind up here was sharply cooler than in the lower meadow, where they had worked all day. Nevertheless, they sweated through their tee shirts and cursed the job with each breath of the thin air.

After the sun went down behind the mountain, they climbed back into the truck. This time Milo was driving, and, even with the Jeep in lowest gear, he had to work the brakes constantly.

"No wonder we're tired, Milo," Ted panted. "It's damn high up here!"

They came to the stream that crossed the upper meadow, slowed the Jeep to a crawl, and then stopped. Dad had shut the gate to keep the range cows out of the alfalfa.

"It's your turn, Ted," Milo said.

They had been taking turns opening and closing various gates all summer. One of them would unlatch and swing it out of the way while the other drove through, then move it back and hold it taut to reattach the wire loop.

Ted, who was slouched down in the passenger seat with a hat over his face, simply said, "You wanna go to Elko?"

"But it's your *turn*, Ted."

"Yeah, but it's my *car* we're driving to Elko."

"That's not fair. It's your turn."

"Milo, you wanna go to Elko?"

Finally, when they heard the dinner bell in the distance, Milo relented. He jumped out of the truck and ran toward the gate.

In the 1960s, Elko, Nevada, a hub for surrounding ranches, was the only decent place to stay east of Reno on what is now U.S. 80. One late summer afternoon, three young boys in inner tubes tossed a large rubber ball among themselves in the Thunderbird Motel's kidney-shaped swimming pool.

"OK!" shouted a voice coming through the gate. "Everybody out!"

The boys turned their gaze on a dark-haired man wearing black horned-rimmed glasses and carrying a clipboard under his arm. Behind him came a tall, blond teenager in red swim trunks, tanned muscles rippling in the sun.

"This guy's training for the Olympics," said the man with the glasses, "and he needs to do his time trials."

The blond ambled over to a chaise lounge, where he tossed his towel. He turned to stare at the boys.

The kids splashed out of different sides of the pool and ran to the far end of the concrete deck, dragging their inner tubes. The teenager bent down, retrieved the red ball, and casually threw it over to where they were huddled under one giant beach towel. Their eyes followed him in anticipation as he walked onto the diving board.

The man with the glasses took out a stop watch, held up his arm, waited a few seconds, then lowered his hand in a sweeping arc as he cried, "Go!"

There was an explosion as the swimmer hit the water, and in seconds he was touching the other side of the pool. He flipped over and started across again, a rhythmic ballet of strength and grace. Up and down he swam. Four laps, six, ten.

The man with the glasses finally called out, "Time!" He wrote something on his clipboard.

"Milo," he yelled, "only three seconds short of your all-time record!"

The boys looked at each other, then watched as the swimmer repeated his feat twice more, each time shaving off another "official" second. As people came through the gate wearing swim suits, they were chastised by the oldest boy not to use the pool.

"That guy's training for the Olympics," he warned. "You gotta wait 'till he breaks his record!"

Later, as Ted and Milo walked across the street for the buffet at the Centennial Casino, Milo smirked, "That's one way to have the pool all to ourselves!"

~~~

The people who seem most prone to develop bipolar illness are those who have an outgoing temperament. They are responsive to other people, and their enthusiasm and sense of fun can be very engaging. They can be carefree, sociable, and highly energetic ...

– *Depression and Bipolar Disorders,* by Virginia Edwards, Your Personal Health Series, Firefly Books (U.S.) Inc., 2002, p. 44. Reprinted with permission of Key Porter Books. Copyright © by Virginia Edwards

[In mania] delusions or hallucinations may emerge, although the manic-depressive might not tell anyone [he or she] is hearing voices or seeing religious figures, UFOs, or other sights. Delusions are thoughts or feelings sincerely felt that are simply untrue. [They] can include grandiose beliefs; a person may think [he or] she has special skills or talents, or is related to a famous person.

– *We Heard the Angels of Madness: A Family Guide to Coping with Manic Depression*, by Diane & Lisa Berger, William Morrow & Company, 1991, p. 47

Chapter Seven: Signs of Trouble

September 1963

The August days were growing shorter. Aspen trees along the stream were turning from silver-green to yellow, and the last cutting of alfalfa lay in wait for the mower. A cool breeze blew across the valley. For the first morning all summer, a fire was lit in the living room.

Carolyn and Milo were packing up for school. They would attend the University of Nevada in Reno. It was Carolyn's third year, Milo's first.

Milo had graduated from Austin High School the previous June. After moving here two years before, he had quickly become the school's prize athlete in basketball and track, even breaking the state record in the 440 event. His grades, though not the highest in his class, were high enough to meet the requirements of a state university. Oscar and Charlotte were thankful for the low tuition. They had been running the ranch on a shoestring, fixing their own equipment, putting off needed improvements, and hoping cattle prices would rise.

It had been a summer of hard work. At this altitude, the growing season was short. A couple of storms, trouble with the bailer, and Dad's broken shoulder as a result of being bucked off a mustang horse, had held up progress on putting up the hay. But the final "Golden Bale" had been placed atop the haystack just yesterday.

There had also been visitors, old friends and family from Southern California. One of those was Frank, a co-worker of Oscar's from Northrup Aviation, who had flown up in his single-engine airplane to help Oscar fix some of the equipment.

That afternoon, when he heard the drone of the engine, Milo was into the old Jeep pickup and leaving a trail of dust before the plane landed on the dirt road down the valley. After Milo helped secure the small aircraft with chocks and rope, they put Frank's suitcase in the Jeep. Frank patiently answered Milo's endless questions on the way to the house. What was it like to fly in mountainous country? How much horsepower did Frank's Tailorcraft have? What was its top airspeed? How many hours did it take to learn to fly?

At breakfast the next morning, Milo talked Frank into taking him up in the plane. Frank said he would allow Milo to handle the controls for a few minutes. Milo poked at a pancake while Frank finished his coffee.

As Milo slammed the screen door he called to Oscar, "Leave that mowing for me—I'll do it when I get back."

That night, as everyone munched corn from Charlotte's vegetable garden, Frank muttered something about a close call; he talked about dangerous downdrafts in the high mountains of the Great Basin. When asked for more detail, it was Milo who changed the subject.

After Frank left, Milo was subdued, quiet, not his jovial self at mealtimes. No wisecracks about that last elusive "Golden

Bale" of the summer or witty vignettes in the saga of "Joe the Irrigator" and his nemesis, *gopherus gigantus*.

One morning, Oscar discovered a flat tire on the cattle truck and asked Milo to change it. As Oscar worked nearby, sharpening the scythe for the mower, he noticed that Milo was putting in the lug nuts backward, leaving the screw ends sticking outwards.

"*He knows better than that*," Oscar thought to himself, as he continued to watch out of the corner of his eye. Soon, Milo became aware of his mistake and reluctantly took out the lug nuts and put them in correctly.

As Charlotte was cleaning Milo's room that afternoon, she noticed a piece of notebook paper under the bed. Stooping to pick it up, she recognized Milo's familiar printing, more scrawled than usual. It was the title of the poem that alarmed her.

I am Jesus Christ
by
Milo John Reese

How else could I fly like the wind?
I lift all mankind on my wings
Sins forgiven, we soar over
The evil wasteland below
Aim toward Paradise
And watch as fire
Engulfs The
World.

That September day came when the kids had to leave. It had taken Charlotte hours to iron Milo's shirts and pants with the flat irons heated up on the back of the woodstove. The old Ford was filled to the brim with clothes, books, pillows, and blankets. After shooing the old cat, Tobey, from the top of the pile in the back seat, Carolyn and Milo said their goodbyes and drove slowly down the washboard driveway. The leaves on the poplar trees swirled off in the increasing wind.

Oscar and Charlotte watched them go. They saw Milo get out to open the gate, then wait as Carolyn drove through. There was a honk from the horn as they disappeared around the bend behind the first hill.

~~~

Although hallucinations may affect all senses, they usually are imagined sights or sounds. Auditory hallucinations are more common and may have a religious overtone, such as the voice of God or angels, and may sound like commands.
  – *We Heard the Angels of Madness*: *A Family Guide to Coping with Manic Depression*, by Diane & Lisa Berger, William Morrow & Company, New York, 1991, p. 47

The high level of stress in our society is especially relevant to bipolar sufferers because…stress can sometimes play a part in triggering episodes of mania, hypomania, or depression. Stress is defined in two ways: It can refer to a situation that puts a large number of difficult demands on us, and it can also refer to the feelings that such situations generate.
– *Coping with Bipolar Disorder: A Guide to Living with Manic Depression,* by Steven Jones, Peter Hayward, Dominic Lam, Oneworld Publications, 2002

Chapter Eight: Christmas at the Callahan

December 1963

Whatever the circumstances, Mom had always made Christmas special. This year, preparations began earlier than usual, and late nights were spent with the Montgomery Ward catalogue. Orders would have to be made at least two months ahead to make sure they would arrive at the Austin Post Office in time for her to sneak into town by herself to pick them up. Gifts would be needed items such as a warm jacket for Milo and boots for Dad. She would have to forgo the expensive candied cherries and walnuts for her fruit breads. The cows came first, and they usually had a veto on any extras in the budget.

* * *

When Ted and I pulled up to the snow-laden house on Christmas Eve, we could smell rich memories of Mom's anise cookies mingling with the aroma of onion and sage for the turkey stuffing. (No mutton for this lady's Christmas dinner!)

Muldoon ran out with a welcoming bark. We could see Carolyn's old Ford parked by the barn. She and Milo came out to greet us. After hugs and banter about how many hours the trip had taken from Santa Barbara (eleven), did we stop to put on chains (yes), and had we heard that new group called The Beatles (we hadn't), they helped us carry our bags and gifts into the house.

Milo gave Ted their now-standard greeting, "You wanna go to Elko?"

We asked Carolyn and Milo how school was going. Carolyn was eager to tell us all about her classes, her job, and her friends.

To our questions, Milo just answered, "Fine."

As I carried my suitcase into the back bedroom, Carolyn pulled me aside.

"I'm really worried about Milo," she said. "I heard from another student that he was flunking most of his classes, and he's been acting weird lately."

"But Milo is really smart," I offered.

"Maybe," she said. "But I just don't think he can handle college. Don't say anything to Mom yet. I'll try to keep an eye on him."

Early Christmas morning, while Ted slept in, Dad and Milo left to feed the cows. Mom and I were washing the breakfast dishes when we heard the rifle shot. Carolyn ran into the kitchen.

"What was that?" she asked.

"It sounded like it came from the lower meadow," I said. Mom dried her hands, and the three of us went out on the front porch, where the thermometer read twelve degrees. We stood there shivering.

The hay wagon was a few hundred yards away, silhouetted in the rising sun down toward the eastern fence. No sound from the tractor. Cows formed an ellipse where the hay had been dropped, their heads down, chewing with purpose.

Two figures carried something over to the empty bed of the wagon. One of them stepped up onto the tractor. Now we could hear the familiar sound of the John Deere motor as it slowly made its way back toward the barn.

Ted was at the dining table eating pancakes when Milo and Dad came through the door. They unpeeled their jackets, gloves and hats and hung them up on pegs along the wall.

"Was that a gunshot?" Mom asked as she poured coffee and cocoa for them.

"I had to shoot Muldoon this morning," Dad said. "We found him down by the east fence just after he'd killed a calf."

We looked at each other. Milo's cocoa was still untouched.

"There was nothing else to do." Dad continued. "Once they get the taste of blood, they'll do it again and again."

That night, we played a few hands of poker and watched the snow come down through the blackness of the dining room window. I knew Ted was concerned that we might be snowed in, but I was secretly delighted at the prospect.

"We had wonderful fall weather up until just three weeks ago," Mom said.

"Yeah," Milo responded. "Dad even gave me some flying lessons."

"You're kidding." I looked at Dad.

"I have a friend in town," Dad said, as he dealt another hand of cards. "He's a mechanic that works on my equipment once in a while. He has a small plane. Parks it at an airstrip on the other side of Austin. He lent it to us a few times."

"What grade did you give him, Oscar?" Ted asked.

"A-plus! Milo's a natural-born pilot."

"Tell us a flying story, Dad," Milo said. Ted had won all the hands of poker, and we were finishing up the mince pie.

"Well, let's see." Dad leaned back in his chair and scratched his forehead. "There was the time I was testing a B-17. We were over Palmdale, going along fine. Then I happened to look down, and I noticed that the floor was six inches deep in gasoline."

"Egad. What did you do, Dad?"

"I called the guy that was riding in the tail gunner seat and asked him what he thought. He said I should land the plane immediately. But I was worried that the friction and bouncing around on touch-down would set that stuff off. I thought of other alternatives; each seemed impossible — except maybe bailing out.

"Suddenly, I knew what to do. I opened the Bombay doors, and the gasoline dropped out."

"Didn't it come in contact with sparks from the engines?" Milo asked.

"No. The force of the wind whipped the gas behind the plane."

"Bet that guy in the tail wondered what in the hell you were doing."

"Actually, the gas got his bubble cleaner than it had ever been."

I looked at Milo. He was staring long-distance out the window, through the falling snow, tapping his foot. He had a warped smile on his face.

On the trip back to Santa Barbara, I told Ted what Carolyn had said about Milo.

"I hope he doesn't drop out of college," I mused. "Maybe he's been having too much fun, you know, drinking, going to parties, like we used to do."

"I think it's more than that." Ted slowed the car to maneuver through the slush on the highway. "He seems almost like he's 'flying high.'"

~~~

Bipolar disorder in...adolescents competes with channeling cognitive and emotional energies essential for academic achievement. The older adolescent may have extreme difficulty continuing school ... Although a bipolar child may be extremely bright and creative in certain areas, bipolar illness interferes

with a child's capacity to master skills or meet the challenges associated with normal emotional and social development.
– *New Hope for People with Bipolar Disorder*, by Jan Fawcett, M.D., Bernard Golden, Ph.D., Nancy Rosenfeld, copyright 2000 by Jan Fawcett, Bernard Golden, and Nancy Rosenfeld. Used by permission of Prima Publishing, a division of Random House, Inc.

Bipolar disorder seems usually to be first diagnosed when the person affected is in the later teenage or early adult years. One major review of age of onset suggested that the highest risk period is in people between fifteen and twenty-four years.
 — *Coping with Bipolar Disorder: A Guide to Living with Manic Depression*, by Steven Jones, Peter Hayward, & Dominic Lam, Oneworld Press, 2002

Chapter Nine: The Phone Call

April 1964

In 1964, the campus of the University of Nevada in Reno boasted a small collection of two-story brick buildings and one football stadium. The brown grass and bare aspen trees belied the fact that it was early spring. Although the days were getting longer, there was still frost at night.

Carolyn and some of her friends sat in the dining commons one evening after dinner, drinking coffee. They were putting off the inevitable walk back to the dorm to study for their midterms this week.

"Are you gonna stay here in Reno this summer and work? I hear the Frontier is hiring."

"Yeah. Are you? Maybe we can room together."

"I'll have to go to summer school if I don't start cramming on the books."

"Hey, Carolyn, isn't that your brother?"

Carolyn turned as Milo came toward her. His red-rimmed eyes were filled with terror. He'd never looked at her this way before. His hair was wild. He wore no jacket, even though the temperature outside was in the twenties.

"Carolyn!"

He gave the urgent command again. "Carolyn!"

"What?"

He seemed not to hear her response.

Over and over again: "Carolyn! Carolyn!"

"Milo, have you had dinner?"

"Carolyn!"

"What's the matter, Milo?"

The other girls at the table shrank back in their seats. One by one, they put on their coats and left. Carolyn sat staring after Milo as he finally turned and strode through the back door into the night. She wondered if she should call Mom and Dad.

Two longs, one short. Charlotte rolled over in bed. The phone on the wall in the dining room was ringing. What time was it? Again: two longs, one short.

"That's our ring," she said, as she shivered out of bed and groped for her frayed terrycloth slippers. Oscar stirred, turned over in his bed and soon resumed his snoring in a steady rhythm.

Charlotte grabbed the flashlight on the nightstand, turned it on and aimed it at the clock. Two-thirty. She stumbled through to the next room as the insistent ringing continued. Her sister? Oscar's mother? Who had died?

She grabbed the receiver and shouted, "Hello?" One had to talk loudly to be heard on these rural phones. The voice on the other end grew more faint with each click of another person on the line picking up to listen in.

"Is this Charlotte Reese? Mother of Milo John Reese?"

"Yes, it is. Who is this?"

"I'm calling from Washoe Medical Center in Reno."

Charlotte steadied herself on the arm of the rocker and slowly sank into its worn cushion as she choked out her question.

"What's happened? Is Milo all right?"

The backs of her knees began to crawl.

"Your son was brought here by the Reno Police Department after being picked up by the campus police at the University. He was demonstrating bizarre behavior."

"Bizarre behavior?"

"He was walking around for several days talking to himself. Then they found him trying to break into some parked cars outside his dorm."

"Did he hurt himself? Is that why he's in the hospital?"

"He's physically fine, but we're detaining him here in the psychiatric ward. We won't know what's really wrong with him until we do some tests, but his symptoms indicate some kind of severe mental illness."

"But…I don't believe it. I…"

"Have there been previous episodes of strange behavior, Mrs. Reese?"

"No. Ugh…" Charlotte's mind raced back over the recent months, remembering the poem she had found under his bed.

And Charlotte realized now what she had always known, on some level, from the time Milo was three or four. He was "different." Not just different in gender from her girls, but from other little boys, too. She had never put her finger on it, even though she had taken many psychology courses as a nursery school teacher. Overdue motor skills. Night terrors. His delayed verbal abilities. Later, a frantic drive to achieve. His strange disappearances.

And she remembered that, when he was in his teens, there would sometimes be a scent about him, different from sweat or dirty socks. A scent that alarmed her, that seemed somehow chemical. Everything seemed to fall heavily into place now.

~~~

In everyday life, the subjective turmoil we associate with stress is not inherently harmful … [However,] stressful situations that create personal turmoil commonly precede episodes of depression and mania … Furthermore, it is

repeated stress or chronic stress, where control over the situation has been lost or given up...that seems to be particularly malignant in the kindling of bipolar illness.

– *A Mood Apart: The Thinker's Guide to Emotion and its Disorders*, by Peter C. Whybrow, M.D., Harper-Perrenial, A Division of HarperCollins Publishers, by arrangement with Perseus Basic Books, 1997

A typical manic episode from beginning to end was described after one research study as a desperate, panic stricken, hopeless state experienced by the patient as clearly [unpleasant], accompanied by frenzied and frequently ever more bizarre... activity. Thought processes that earlier had been only difficult to follow now became incoherent ... Delusions were bizarre... hallucinations were present in some patients.
— National Institutes of Health, 1973

Chapter Ten: Flipping Out

May 1964

Besides Dr. Brown, there were two orderlies in the room. The patient, a young adult male, had been brought to the Nevada state mental hospital after a month at Washoe Medical Center. He was being treated for what had been diagnosed as schizophrenia after a complete mental breakdown during his first year at the University of Nevada. His name was Milo John Reese, aged nineteen, six feet tall, one hundred fifty-five pounds. He lay quietly but held a wide-eyed gaze upward and stared at the ceiling above.

"Can you hear me, son? I'm Dr. Brown. We're going to put a couple of straps on you so you can't hurt yourself during this procedure. Then I'll be injecting you with a mild sedative. O.K.?"

As two of the orderlies began to secure the leather straps on his arms, the patient suddenly arched his back and sprang upwards. He leaped off the table. Before anyone could restrain him, there was an explosion of glass as he crashed through the large second-story window and jumped to the patio below.

"I can't understand it," Dr. Brown mused afterward. "He went through a plate glass window, down two stories, and onto concrete. All that and only a bruise on his left arm. It was like he was superhuman."

"And pretty darn lucky," said one of the orderlies.

"What about the shock treatments?" Mom asked. "Must he still have them?"

"I think we'll wait on those for awhile. We'll continue the Thorazine for now."

Three weeks later, after Milo had been discharged from the hospital, Mom called Dr. Brown.

"Doctor, Milo is not doing well at all," Mom said. "He's talking to himself again, and he doesn't respond to anything we say to him."

"Double the Thorazine," responded Dr. Brown.

An hour later, there was another call.

"Doctor," said his nurse, "it's Mrs. Reese again. She sounded pretty frantic this time."

"Yes, Mrs. Reese."

"Doctor, Milo has passed out. I don't know what to do!"

"You'd better bring him in, then."

"OK, but, you know, we're almost two hundred miles from Reno."

"Put him in the back seat of your car. Make him comfortable. And hurry!"

As they drove into the outskirts of Reno, Mom looked into the back seat. Milo's eyes had rolled back into his head.

"Carolyn," she shouted, "hit the gas! I don't think he's breathing!"

Carolyn speeded up the car.

Mom screamed, "Faster! Faster!"

That night, they sat in the waiting room, drinking coffee and smoking Carolyn's Parliaments. This was Mom's first cigarette in twenty years. Finally, Dr. Brown came out. His face was sober.

"You got him here just in time, Mrs. Reese. Milo's going to be O.K. But he seems to be intolerant of Thorazine. We'll have to try something else."

And thus began a long journey through the maze of mental illness.

~~~

The dopamine agents (commonly known as neuroleptics and principally used in the treatment of schizophrenia) are widely employed to decrease excitement and to control racing thoughts. Chlorpromazine [brand name Thorazine, developed in the early 1950s], Thioridazine, Trifluroperazine, and Haloperidol are among the most commonly used. All of these drugs are extremely potent and cause many side effects, including…sedation, low blood pressure and a fast heart rate.

– *A Mood Apart: The Thinker's Guide to Emotion and its Disorders*, by Peter C. Whybrow, M.D., Harper-Perennial, a Division of HarperCollins Publishers, 1998, pp. 265-266

Part Four:

Turbulent Years

Villon, our sad bad glad mad brother's name.
   – Algernon Charles Swinburne, *A Ballad of Francois Villon*

Alone

by

Milo John Reese

Just a fickle robin,
 a wind swirling by,
nothing here is still,
 emptiness soars high.

I stand alone
 in wilderness,
imagining peace
 within nurtured bliss.

This mothering soil,
 below a father tree,
sprouts suckling flowers.
 Tenderness I see.

A hand was here
 from which these seeds were sown.
I look again.
 Was I alone?

—

1982

Symptoms [of depression] include a persistent sad mood; loss of interest or pleasure in activities that were once enjoyed; significant change in appetite or body weight; difficulty sleeping or oversleeping; physical slowing or agitation; loss of energy; feelings of worthlessness or inappropriate guilt; difficulty thinking or concentrating; and recurrent thoughts of death or suicide. The depressive episodes of people with bipolar disorder are often indistinguishable from those of patients with unipolar major depressive disorder.
    – *Bipolar Disorder Research at the National Institute of Mental Health: Fact Sheet,* Print version, 2004, http://www.nimh.nih.gov/publicat/bipolarresfact.cfm

Chapter Eleven: The Shady Rest Motel

May 1972

Ted drove around Palmdale for an hour before he found it. It was on a street just off the Antelope Valley Freeway, on what used to be the main route through town. The Shady Rest Motel now sat nestled in a sea of weeds. On one side was a junk yard; on the other, a plumbing supply store.

Ted pulled in by the sign marked "Office." He noticed only one other car, way in the back, and he guessed that it hadn't been driven in years. It looked like an old Mercury, the kind they made in the fifties, the body overloaded with chrome. The chrome was rust-colored now, its sun-baked paint almost unrecognizable in color, its tires all flat.

The door to the office squeaked open to Ted's shove. There was no one behind the dust-covered counter, but he could hear the sound of a TV through the wall. He hit the round bell twice. And again. Finally, there came a shuffling noise from the back room. The door marked "Private" opened, and there stood one of the fattest men Ted had ever seen. Squeezing himself through the door, the man peered over his half glasses.

"We don't get many customers at one thirty in the afternoon," he said. There was the distinct smell of bourbon on his breath.

"I'm not here for a room," Ted said. "I came to get my brother-in-law. He's supposed to be staying here. His name is Milo John Reese."

"Oh, yeah." The man scratched the stubble on his chin. "If he's still here, he's in seventeen. He was wandering around earlier. Acting kind of strange, too. He was talking to himself."

A few minutes later, Ted knocked on the door of room 17. "Milo? You here?"

"Who is it?" Milo's voice was barely recognizable.

"Open up, Milo. It's Teddy. I've come to get you." Then the familiar greeting, "You wanna go to Elko?"

The door finally opened. Milo's light brown hair was plastered to his forehead. He wore a filthy tee-shirt, and his blue eyes were glazed and bloodshot. "No kidding? You came all the way from Santa Barbara?"

"Yes," Ted answered. "Your mom and dad asked me to come get you. I'll take you home with me, then we'll figure a way to get you back to Reno."

"Okay."

"We'll also take you to a doctor and get you some medication."

"No, don't need any medication."

During the long drive north, Ted failed to coax more than a few words from his passenger.

"What happened to your car, Milo?"

"Bishop."

"It broke down there?"
"Yeah."
"How did you get to Palmdale?"
"Bus."

For most of the hundred-mile trip to Santa Barbara, Milo's face was in constant motion, forming all manner of agonized expressions. His tortured eyes stared at some distant point on the road ahead.

Meanwhile, at home, I paced around the house and waited. Milo's doctor in Reno had called us with a referral to a psychiatrist in Santa Barbara. When Ted and Milo arrived, we immediately contacted his office. Since this was an emergency, the nurse said we could come right in.

The doctor talked to Milo for a few minutes, did a basic physical exam, then wrote a prescription. He made Milo take two pills immediately.

That night, we fed Milo some dinner and watched while he took the next dose of the medicine we had picked up at the pharmacy. Lithium Carbonate. After putting him to bed in our spare room, Ted and I watched TV until two a.m., keeping some sort of vigil.

When he awoke the next morning, Milo was hungry for breakfast, and his grimace was gone.

A few days later, we put him on a bus to Reno. He promised that he would keep taking his pills, then smiled and waved goodbye through the dirty window as he slid into his seat near the back.

~~~

"The real challenge about bipolar disorder is that we are either treating mania or we are treating depression, but we have always got to keep in mind what the liabilities of treatments might be for the other pole of the illness …When we treat bipolar depression, are we going to be using a medication such as a unimodal antidepressant agent, that has the liability for inducing mania or rapid cycling?"

– Mark Frye, M.D., at a recent meeting of the U.S. Psychiatric and Mental Health Congress in San Diego, citing a study at the Huston Health Science Center in 2001

Persons with psychiatric conditions are too often regarded as untreatable and thus unpredictable and dangerous, or at the very least unreliable and incompetent. Too many films and television programs still ridicule or demonize individuals with psychiatric illnesses, and words like *crazy* **and** *insane* **are generalized terms of contempt that you can hear in any schoolyard during recess.**
– *Bipolar Disorder: A Guide for Patients and Families*, by Francis Mark Mondimore, M.D., Johns Hopkins University Press, 1999, pp. 230-231

Chapter Twelve: Friends and Family

After that first psychotic break, during his first and only year in college, Milo would be "well" for awhile, perhaps six months or a year. But, at some point, the mania would recur and, with it, Milo would get the urge to travel.

I was reluctant to share the fact of my brother's illness with friends, as was Carolyn. We were afraid that it would stigmatize us in their eyes, and they might wonder if and when we ourselves might go crazy.

But by now, most of our relatives knew about Milo. It was the early 1970s, and they, like most people at that time, were still terrified of anything "psychological," especially any label which implied "psychotic" behavior symptoms. They would conclude that the stricken person was surely a mass murderer and try to distance themselves. Perhaps this was one reason the whole situation was so hard on our parents, especially our father.

In 1972, Milo met a female patient during one of his stays in the mental hospital. One night they went out the back door, found a Reno wedding chapel, and had a five-minute ceremony.

After Milo and his wife were released, they honeymooned in San Francisco. At the time, I wondered how they could afford it. Several months later, I learned that they had stayed with our uncle in his home near the city. Milo must have loved that trip, because several months later, I received a call from Uncle Ray.

"Hello?"

"Cynthia!" His anger cut into my ear as I held the phone in the crook of my neck. I was trying to peel a cucumber and keep my eye on the clock. We had guests coming for dinner, and I barely had enough time left to take a shower.

"Well, what do I do if he shows up here?" Ray asked.

"Call the police if you're scared, Ray," I suggested.

I doubted he would take my advice. Ray lived in a fancy neighborhood, and he would probably be worried about how it would look to have a patrol car drive up.

"His postcard is marked Reno." Ray had not heard a word I said. "Dated last Friday: 'Dear Uncle Raymond'—I've told him a thousand times to call me Ray, and without the Uncle! 'We thought we'd take a few days vacation and see the sights in Frisco.' Doesn't he know that this city is called *San Francisco*? He says here, 'We'd like to stay at your place again, if that's O.K...' Well, it isn't O.K. *at all*."

"I don't know what to tell you, Ray. You could try to call him, but I don't think he has a phone now. And he's probably already on the road anyway ..."

"The last time they were here," Ray went on, "they ate me out of house and home. No one lifted a finger to help me in the kitchen. And then I had to give him gas money to get them to leave!"

"I know, Ray ..."

"And now, this time," Ray said through clenched teeth, "maybe *he* has a job—what is it, digging ditches? But s*he's* right out of the *hospital! Again! A*nd they're both crazy to start with!"

"I am sorry this has got you so upset, Ray. But I'm not my brother's keeper."

"Well, if he comes, I'll just pretend I'm not home."

"Good idea, Ray."

I hung up the phone and walked toward the bathroom, ripping off my clothes and stuffed them into the hamper. Under the shower, I could feel my heartbeat through the taut muscles in my neck as I washed my hair.

~~~

With ongoing conditions such as SMI [Severe Mental Illness]…friends and family may not find any closure on their grieving process … These illnesses thus create agony not only for the stricken but for their entire family. We lose our original relationships with SMI relatives, as well as our dreams and beliefs about their futures.

– *The Skipping Stone: Ripple Effects of Mental Illness on the Family*, by Mona Wasow, Clinical Professor, Science & Behavior Books, Inc., Palo Alto, CA., 1995, pp. 103-105

Why does a major psychiatric disorder such as manic-depressive illness tend to concentrate in a relatively limited number of families? ... It may have to do with "assortative mating," the tendency for men and women with psychiatric conditions to be attracted to and marry each other.
   – *A Brilliant Madness: Living with Manic-Depressive Illness*, by Patty Duke and Gloria Hochman, Bantam Books, 1992

Chapter Thirteen: Crescent City

June 1973

"Hey, it's us! Surprise! Surprise!"

"Mom! Dad! I thought you were in New Mexico!"

"We were," announced Mom. "But we decided to cut it short. We're on our way to see Milo in Crescent City."

"And little Kevin." Dad said as he half turned, gesturing at the street. Parked by the curb were his pickup truck and a small travel trailer. "And we want you and Ted to come with us! We'll camp on the way."

My parents had recently sold the ranch. They were in the process of looking for another place to live. Meanwhile, Milo and his wife had moved to Northern California, where her parents lived. Milo worked at a construction job there, and they had a new baby boy.

"But Dad, I have all these projects going on ..."

"Teachers have the whole summer off, right? We'll be back in a week or so."

"Yes, but …"

Ted came out of the bedroom, rubbing his eyes. "Oscar. Charlotte. Hi! I thought I heard voices out here."

"We're here to talk you and Cynthia into going with us to see Milo."

Outnumbered, I soon gave in, and we set about to get ready for the trip. We asked the young girl up the street to feed the cats. I started throwing some old tee-shirts and jeans into a suitcase. We found our sleeping bags in the garage, and Ted was airing them out in the driveway as he gave the yard a good watering.

Shortly after lunch, the house was locked up and we climbed into the pickup. Ted and Dad rode in the front seat; Mom and I sat in patio chairs in the camper shell.

"I didn't have time to buy the baby a gift," I said to Mom as I stared through the smudged window at the rolling hills, already golden in mid-June.

"What they really need is money. For basics, like diapers or formula."

"She's really loony, isn't she, Milo's wife?" I asked. "Sicker than he is, right?"

"Well, she was diagnosed with schizophrenia, just like he was, but I understand there might have been a couple of bouts of LSD in there, too."

"Not while she was pregnant, surely."

"Yes, I'm afraid so."

"What's going to happen to this baby, with two mental patients for parents?"

"God only knows."

Two days later, with stops at Half Moon Bay and The Redwoods, we pulled into the fog of Crescent City. I snuggled into my jacket. Even inside the truck the dampness permeated everything. The harbor was true to the map, crescent shaped. We could see fishing boats coming in through the mist.

"Oscar was talking about taking Milo fishing while we're here," Mom said.

"Remember the other time we came here on a family vacation?" I asked. "The time we stayed in your friend's house and we all went out in that little boat. Milo caught a huge salmon."

"Yes. We had it smoked and ate it all the way home. Milo was only seven then. Dad helped him reel in the fish. I also remember picking blueberries, and you kids were so frustrated because it took two hours just to fill one small basket."

"But they were sure good, weren't they? Maybe we can do that again. And there are probably tours of the old lighthouse."

We found a campground outside of town. Mom and I set out the kerosene stove and lantern on the red and white tablecloth. Dad and Ted went to find a phone. A few minutes later, we all piled into the truck again. We had been invited to Milo's for dinner.

The visit is fragmented in my mind. I remember a tiny, one bedroom old house in which they all lived: Milo, his wife, his mother-in-law, father-in-law, and the baby. Milo's wife's mother worked at a fish factory, and her calloused hands were the color of shrimp from peeling them all day.

The only thing I remember about our meal there is that there were shrimp. Mountains of them. Our hands also became red as we helped clean them.

A red-haired baby lay crying in an old crib. When Mom picked him up, he was quiet. I noticed that his blue-green eyes were crossed. The house smelled of dirty diapers. The father-in-law was on the couch in his undershirt, a beer in his hand. The mother-in-law drank Muscatel as she doused the crustaceans into the pot of boiling water on the stove. A small woman with pale skin, Milo's wife sat at the small kitchen table staring out the window.

Milo, eyes ringed with fatigue, finally came home from work. He said he was working a lot of overtime now because it rained here so much in the winter. When he reached to hug me, I saw the distant look in his eyes.

Milo's mother-in-law got out some smudged juice glasses and passed around the wine. Dad and Mom declined. Ted and I held our glasses but didn't drink.

The next morning, Dad announced that he thought we should leave. The three of us nodded our heads in agreement. No one mentioned plans to go fishing.

As we pulled out of the campground, I turned to Mom and asked, "How can they live in those conditions? How can Milo stand it? His wife is a zombie, her parents are drunks …"

"I think Milo's getting sick again," Mom confided. "Your father sees the signs, too. That's why he wanted to leave. This illness scares the heck out of him."

"It scares the heck out of *all* of us," I said.

~~~

But no matter what the form or severity of the symptoms, the families of those who are manic-depressive suffer emotions as intense and racking as those experienced by the victims of the disease. They leapfrog from empathy to exasperation, from anxiety to anger, from fear to frustration … Whatever the scenario, for every person who is manic-depressive, there are multiple others in agony.

– *A Brilliant Madness: Living with Manic-Depressive Illness,* by Patty Duke and Gloria Hochman, Bantam Books, 1992, p. 217

With this type of man, [a *puer aeternus*]...there is a highly symbolic fascination for dangerous sports—particularly flying and mountain climbing—so as to get as high as possible, the symbolism being to get away from reality, from the earth, from ordinary life.
 – *The Problem of the Puer Aeternus*, Marie-Louise von Franz (1915-1998), edited by Daryl Sharp, Inner City Books, Copyright 2000, pp. 8-9

Chapter Fourteen: Flying Stories

April 1976

"Tell us another one, Dad." Milo's eyes were bright as he picked out another piece of See's Candy from the box on the lazy Susan. While Mom and I dried dishes, the men sat around the old oak table digesting Easter brunch. They shouted clues to three-year-old Kevin as he ran around the house hunting eggs. It was raining, so we'd hidden the eggs in such places as shower stalls, pillow cases, and shoes.

Oscar and Charlotte had bought land just south of Carson City and built a small home on one of the lots. They would soon sell it and purchase another piece of property on which they could build their "dream house." They were looking at land across the Carson Valley, on the mountain behind the town of Genoa.

At some point, whenever the family was together, Milo would urge Dad to entertain us with tales of his "close calls" as a pilot. I would later comprehend the full meaning of this ritual for Milo.

Milo was now divorced, with full custody of his son. His ex-wife, severely mentally ill, could not control an overactive toddler. Milo had a construction job in Reno, where he and Kevin were living in a rented studio apartment. Mom had told me that the bed they shared took up most of the space in its one room.

"Well, let's see," Dad mused, leaning back in his chair with a deck of cards in his hands, about to deal a hand of poker. "Have I told you this one? I once flew for a non-scheduled airline company for thirty days. I quit because it was a fly-by-night operation ..."

"*Literally* a fly-by-night operation!" said Milo, with a grin.

"Like Mrs. Furguson's Storm Door Airline?" Ted chuckled as he twirled the candy around to his place at the table. "The Bob Newhart comedy bit?"

"Something like that," answered Dad. "This was a few years after the war, in the late forties, and these commercial companies were popping up all over. They bought old C46s and converted them to hold fifty-four passengers.

"On my first run, as the copilot on a flight from L.A. to Kansas City, we were somewhere over New Mexico when the captain leaned over and told me that we had to pick up a passenger at that airport there. He pointed out the window, straight down, and asked me if I would land the plane for him.

"As I banked the plane, I couldn't make out anything except sagebrush and an occasional square of alfalfa. Finally, I saw the runway, what there was of it—it was little more than the size of a driveway."

"I haven't heard this one, Dad," I said over my shoulder.

"*I* have." Milo sat up straighter in his chair, his eyes bright.

"There was a storm coming," Dad continued, "and the plane started to bounce around in the wind. Coming in, I had to put it into a near stall so I wouldn't overshoot the runway. We kept the engines running while the stewardess opened the door and lowered the stairs. One lone passenger ran out of the small hangar, carrying a suitcase and holding on to his hat. He climbed on board, the stewardess pulled up the stairs and closed the door, and we took off again."

"Wow," Milo half said, half laughed. "Sounds like the kind of airline *I* should apply for!"

After a few hands of poker, Milo begged for more.

"Another time," Dad said, "on that same L.A. to Kansas City route, we got over Amarillo and the gas gauges read 'Empty.' I suggested to the pilot that we land somewhere and buy some gas. He glanced over and said, 'Nah, we'll make it.'"

"And you did, Dad?" Milo chuckled.

"When we got to the airport in Kansas City, the engines started to sputter. We didn't have enough gas to make a pass around the field, so we had to go straight in.

"As we came in over the runway, all of a sudden we realized that the landing gear wasn't coming down. I don't know what possessed me. I didn't even ask the captain. I just pushed the prop pitch controls all the way forward. These controls, I later found out, regulate the hydraulic system that operates the landing gear."

Milo turned to Ted. "I told you Dad was the greatest pilot of the century!" His smile faded. To Dad, he said, "God must have spoken to you at that very moment."

Milo had recently been "born again." He never missed a Bible study session or Sunday service at the Baptist church he had joined in Reno.

"Just when we were about to touch the runway," Dad went on, "the wheels came down, and we had a perfect three-point landing. The passengers got off the plane and never knew there was a problem. Afterward, I checked the fuel tanks. Empty. I couldn't even smell gas fumes."

Kevin wobbled in, balancing his basket full of eggs, squealing, "All full!"

Mom carefully counted out the eggs. "I just don't want to find one in the back of the closet in mid-July," she muttered.

"Tell 'em the one about the guy that *jumped*, Dad." Milo winked at Ted.

"That was the time I was flying for another airline, also as a copilot. This one just went to cities in California. They flew smaller planes, like DC3s.

"One night, we were coming from Oakland to L.A. All the passengers were asleep back there, except one man who kept asking the stewardess to bring him drinks.

"Finally, he stumbled up to the cockpit and slurred, 'Some guy back there just jumped out!'"

"Cheeeeers!" Milo emphasized the beginning of the word, then drew it out.

"The pilot told the man to go back and sit down and shut up—the stewardess must have been busy with someone else, or she would have intercepted him on his way up the aisle."

Dad took a bite of apple pie. "There was no security then, no cockpit doors.

"We were over the Tehachapi Mountains when this drunk made his way up to the front again. 'Ya gotta' b'leeve me,' he says. 'A guy opened the door and jumped!'

"I offered to go back and check the cabin, but the captain shook his head. He turned to the guy and said, 'I told you to sit down and shut up, Mister!'

"When we taxied in at Burbank, I planned to check the passengers and the manifest, just to be sure. We had barely come to a stop before the stewardess opened the airplane door, lowered the steps, and let all the passengers go.

"I'll never know for certain whether that drunk was telling the truth or not."

Milo smiled, closed his eyes, and turned his head slowly back and forth. Then he broke out in that familiar laugh that had always warmed our hearts.

~~~

The grandiosity of spirit and vision so characteristic of mania, coupled with manic drive and intensity, can add an expansiveness and boldness as well. Under unusual circumstances...this can

result in a formidable combination of imagination, adventurousness, and a restless, quick, and vastly associative mind ...

    – *Touched with Fire: Manic-Depressive Illness and the Artistic Temperament,* by Kay Redfield Jamison, Simon & Schuster, 1993, p. 109

Children of a parent or parents with manic-depressive illness may be profoundly affected by the illness. Even more important, they may think that they are the cause of their parent's illness.
 – *Surviving Manic Depression*, by E. Fuller Torrey, M.D., and Michael B. Knable, D.O., Basic Books, 2002, p. 288

Chapter Fifteen: LAX

April 1981

Rita Carl enjoyed working for Southwest Airlines. She had spent the first five years at the boarding desk in the terminal at Los Angeles International. She had finally arranged her schedule to fit her situation: six a.m. until two p.m., hours in which she didn't have to fight constant fatigue. Most importantly, this shift allowed her to spend time with her twelve-year-old son Darrel when he came home from school. Even help him with his homework. It wasn't easy, being a single parent.

The clocks on the wall gave her the hour in all four time zones in the country. She set her wrist watch to 6:05 L.A. time. Using tissue from the box always kept within reach, she began to wipe off the surface of her space at the counter. *Damn,* she thought, *that guy on the last shift is a pig*—he must have eaten a pizza right here, and without napkins.

Rita looked around the almost deserted waiting area. In half an hour or so, the place would bustle with passengers for the commuter flight to San Francisco. Her eyes darted back to the far corner of the room, where a lone figure sat slumped over two seats. *That guy is sure early*, she thought.

Then, at the edge of her vision, she caught sight of a small boy looking through the debris from an overflowing garbage can next to the now-closed pizzeria stand. As she watched, she saw him open a pizza box, grab a discarded crust, and stuff it into his mouth.

As Rita approached the child, she noticed his dirty face and runny nose. His red hair was in need of a comb. "Hi, little guy. Where's your mommy?" she asked.

"Nah here." Rita could barely understand him. "M' Dad." He pointed toward the slumped figure. The child's blue-green eyes were slightly crossed.

And then it dawned on Rita that she'd seen this same pair in the waiting area yesterday. A tall man in rumpled clothes and a small boy with red hair. He had been staring through the windows at the tarmac. But getting passengers on that last flight of her shift had taken her attention, and she had forgotten about the man and the boy. There was no reason for any passengers to stay overnight in the waiting area—no flights cancelled, no storm conditions anywhere that would affect Southwest flights.

Rita took the boy's hand and led him over to the sleeping man. "Sir, is this your son?" she asked as she gently nudged the man's shoulder. He slowly roused himself.

"Yeah," he said, as he looked out the window past the airplane that sat on the tarmac being equipped for the next flight. Rita noticed the stubble of beard, the worn running shoes, the man's stained shirt.

And an odor, more than that of an unwashed body, a strange aroma of something else, something she couldn't name, something chemical. She grasped the small boy's hand more tightly.

She returned to the reservation desk. She was about to pick up the phone to call the L.A. police department when she noticed the envelope with her name on it. It must have been delivered in the last few minutes. Inside was a note from her boss:

Rita,
  These tickets are for Milo John Reese and his son to use on the next flight to Reno. (They should be somewhere in the passenger wait area.) Reese's father bought them in Nevada. He said not to give Reese the tickets themselves, just to let him board. There will be someone waiting for them at the airport in Reno. Reese has some mental problems, so I wouldn't get him agitated or anything.
      Thanks, T. J.

  Rita went back to the tousled pair just as the first passengers began to arrive. Many were dressed for the business day, with briefcases in hand.
  "Sir," she said to the man called Milo John Reese, "you'll be boarding our ten fifteen flight to Reno. Would you like some coffee? And could I get your son some breakfast?"
  The man continued to stare out through the window, at the lightening gray mist, to where a plane was taking off on the far runway.
  A few weeks later, after Milo was released from the Nevada state mental hospital, I wrote him this letter (in care of my parents):

Dear Milo,
  Mom tells me that you're better now, and that you're on your medications again. She said you're back at work. That's great!
  I sure hope that you will keep taking your pills so this will never happen again. Please consider Kevin and what you have put him through. You are a father now, and your primary responsibility is to your son.
      Love, Cynthia

  The letter was returned to me. My father had opened it and then scrawled this at the bottom:

  I did not give this to Milo. He's sick, remember? Have some compassion, will you?
      Dad

I was stunned by this, and angry about the fact that my brother had never been made to live by the same rules as the rest of us. I felt anguish that now he could ruin his son's life as well as his own by being allowed to pursue whatever his demons told him to do.

Between manic episodes, when he was relatively stable, it was *he,* after all, who made the choice to discontinue his medication. An alcoholic, I reasoned, might or might not have an illness; however, it was the person, not the illness, who made the decision to take that drink.

I tore up the letter.

~~~

Episodes of depression and mania flare up across the life course, often disrupting work, school, family, and social life.
  – Bipolar Disorder Research at the National Institute of Mental Health, Fact Sheet, 6001 Executive Blvd., Room 8185, MSC 9663, Bethesda, Maryland 20892, http://www.nimh.nih.gov

In the early phases of mania, the feelings of power and special ability are compatible—or congruent...with the expansive mood and accelerated thinking. Later, as disorganization clouds normal thinking and memory, suspicion and increased vigilance emerge, perhaps as a last vestige of declining self-awareness and a desperate effort to find explanation.
 – *A Mood Apart: The Thinker's Guide to Emotion and Its Disorders*, by Peter Whybrow, M.D., Harper Perennial, 1998, p. 60

Chapter Sixteen: Trivial Pursuit

December 1982

We were snowed in. The weatherman expected another foot before the storm cleared. From the window in the dining room, I could no longer see ruts in the road that led up the hill. Ted and I had parked down by the water tank when we arrived yesterday; the contours of our car were barely visible now. Although it was only 3:30 in the afternoon, the mountain behind the house, part of the Sierra Nevada range, hid the winter light and gave the illusion of early evening.

This was the first Christmas in Mom and Dad's new home in Genoa. Mom had scrawled "Moved in 10-15-81" on the water heater in the temporary kitchen that was someday meant to be a garage. The house was not finished, but Dad, always in need of a project, was looking forward to doing much of the remaining work himself.

Milo had driven down from Reno late last night after work. He arrived at the house just before the storm hit, honking the horn of his old car as it rumbled up the hill.

"Ho, Ho, Ho!" he'd boomed as we opened the front door. "Merry Christmas!"

There they stood, Milo and little Kevin, shivering in light-weight jackets, wearing neither gloves nor hats. When I had asked Mom what I could get them for gifts, she had told me that they needed some warm clothes.

Milo asked Mom for wrapping paper, and he disappeared into the back bedroom with a large Thrifty's bag and Scotch tape. Although his gifts were always cheap and last-minute, he had an uncanny knack for choosing something we'd appreciate, like the batteries Ted had received last year just after our spare flashlight had burned out. And Carolyn admitted that she always looked forward to the Brach's chocolate-covered cherries.

Later, as Mom and I were putting the silver and china away, Dad played solitaire at the kitchen table. Ted and Milo watched TV in the den. Kevin, making engine noises, rode his new tricycle around and around in the living room.

Carolyn read to her daughters, ages eight and ten, from a book Santa had brought. She was recently divorced, and was teaching at an elementary school at Lake Tahoe. Her gift to Mom and Dad had been a new game, Trivial Pursuit. It was still under the tree.

"Come on, youse guys," I called as I rounded up the family and read the instructions on the back of the box. "There are six of us, not counting kids."

"Exactly the right number of players," said Ted as he took the box from me and read the instructions. "If we're going to be stranded here, and I can't go to the casino, we might as well do something with the time."

We pulled up chairs around the oak table in the kitchen. The lazy Susan was moved away and replaced by the game board.

"Now we'll have the battle of the supreme intellects," said Milo as he winked at Ted.

Carolyn had the directions in her hands as she instructed each of us to select a token and six differently colored plastic wedges.

"Stop that, Milo," Ted said.

"Stop what?" Milo asked.

"That tapping of your knee against the table."

"Oh, you mean *this*?" Milo grinned as he made the table dance with more vigorous blows.

"Very funny," Mom said with a wry smile.

"Each player rolls the die to see who goes first," continued Carolyn. "Then that player rolls the die again and starts from the hub in the center, moving that many spaces towards the outer circle."

"I remember now," Ted nodded his head. "Whatever color box you land on, you're asked a question in that category."

"Right," said Mom, who, as the chosen questioner, had the 1,000 question cards squarely in front of her. "There are six categories: 'Geography,' 'Entertainment,' 'History,' 'Art & Literature,' 'Science & Nature,' 'Sports & Leisure.'"

Milo threw the highest number, a five. "Now watch this," he announced with a grin. "A master at work."

He rolled the die around in his cupped hands with great ceremony, throwing it once again. This advanced his token in an orange box on the board.

"Let's see." Mom reached for the first card. "That's 'Sports and Leisure.' O.K., 'Which U.S. physical education teacher invented basketball?'"

"James Naismith," Milo declared without hesitation.

"Good start, Milo," Ted chided. "However, the really hard questions have yet to come."

An hour later, Milo's token was far ahead of any other on the board. He had collected five of the six colored wedges and was on final approach back to the center to win the game. Besides his ease in answering "Sports & Leisure" questions, Milo demonstrated facility with "Art & Literature." (What Jack Kerouac novel was typed on 120-foot rolls of teletype paper? *On The Road*.)

He showed equal facility in "History" (Who was the top air ace in World War I? *Von Richthofen!*) and "Geography" (How far from Key West is Cuba? *Ninety miles!*)

"Pretty good for only one year of college, eh? Especially against three people with teaching credentials."

Milo rolled the die once more. "And the slaughter continues..."

And it did. "What TV cowboy made Melody Ranch his home?"

"Gene Autry."

"Where was Sarah the only telephone operator?"

"Mayberry."

"Who called Beaver 'Squirt?'"

"Eddie Haskell."

"What's Ricky Nelson's brother's name?"

"David."

"Who played animal behavior expert Professor Ludwig von Complex on *Your Show of Shows*?"

"Sid Caesar."

"I knew all that TV watching would pay off someday." Milo said later as he reached for his prize, the rest of Carolyn's box of Brach's chocolate-covered cherries.

The next morning, Milo came into the kitchen with bloodshot eyes. When Mom offered him breakfast, all he wanted was coffee. He stared straight ahead. As I sat down within his view, it was as if he didn't see me at all.

Kevin was propped on a pillow on one of the kitchen chairs finishing his cereal. He asked, "Can we buy some Cheer'os like these when we get home, Daddy?"

Milo gave no response. Mom let out a long sigh. She said, rather than asked, "Why don't you leave Kevin with us for a few days."

~~~

An experience of dual loss is taking place: of the person who was, and of the person who will never be. Additionally, many

family members share an emphatic grief with the ill relative, whom they sense is also mourning and grieving for his or her own lost hopes and dreams.

— *The Skipping Stone: Ripple Effects of Mental Illness on the Family*, by Mona Wasow, Clinical Professor, Science & Behavior Books, Inc., Palo Alto, CA, 1995, p. 109

The exhilaration and drive that mark the early phases of mania, which is appropriately named hypomania by psychiatrists [the word literally means 'under'-mania], can be easily confused with a joyous celebration of life ... In a happy mood we are expansive and reach out. So it is in hypomania. There is an eagerness to tell others about the good fortune of being alive ... It is this feeling of exhilaration...that is so abundant in hypomania that probably explains its addictive qualities.

– *A Mood Apart,* by Peter C. Whybrow, M.D., HarperPerennial, a Division of HarperCollins Publishers, 1998, pp. 15-16

Chapter Seventeen: Conversions and Conversations

May 1983

The phone was ringing as I laced up my running shoes. Six-fifteen a.m. Maybe it was news about Milo.
"Hello?"
"Well, we found him." It was my mother.
"Is he O.K.? Where's Kevin?"
"They're both all right. They'll be getting on a plane about now, to come back to Reno."
"Back to Reno? Where are they?"
"Miami."
"Miami, *Florida*?"
"That's right."
"How did they get *there*?"

"Well, Milo must have bought two plane tickets—or one, if they let toddlers go free. But when they got to Miami, apparently he realized he didn't have enough money to complete his journey."

"*Complete his journey?*"

"Yes. He told them at the ticket counter there that he was on his way to the Middle East."

"You're kidding."

"They said he mentioned something about walking in the footsteps of Jesus. Anyway, we wired the money for two tickets home. We'll pick them up in Reno. Their plane gets in at 5:15 this afternoon."

"Wow. Poor Mom. What then?"

"Well, if he'll go, we'll take him to the mental hospital, and then we'll bring Kevin back home with us."

"Another adventure, courtesy of Bipolar High Times. Poor Kevin. This has to be rough on a young kid—all these 'adventures.'"

"He probably enjoyed the plane ride."

"Let's hope Milo takes his pills after this."

"I wouldn't hold your breath."

As I hung up the phone, I knew that, once again, Milo's mania had crashed to earth into the quicksand of depression. It was only at these points that he would be amenable to treatment. Once more on medication, he could work again, but sooner or later he would stop the pills. Without these, the illness would inevitably return.

Milo was becoming even more committed to the Christian faith and to the fundamentalist Christian church he had joined. This would lead to a growing number of messianic actions and culminate in his ever-increasing notoriety. The name Milo John Reese was to become familiar to most people in Nevada.

In the 1980s, he was periodically readmitted to the mental facility in Sparks. Sometimes he checked himself in as an outpatient; sometimes he was involuntarily committed on a seventy-two-hour hold. A few stays were several weeks long.

On each occasion, Milo's doctors typically heard complaints of racing thoughts, mood swings, depression, insomnia, and loss of appetite. His demeanor was sometimes cooperative and pleasant, at other times irritable, suspicious, and demanding. Occasionally there were psychotic symptoms such as hallucinations and hearing voices. Milo admitted that he had once thought of suicide and put a gun to his head. To many of the doctors, he denied having mental problems.

In the early course of his illness, Milo had been prescribed Stellazine and other drugs used in treating schizophrenia. Later, when his diagnosis was revised to bipolar disorder, he was given lithium carbonate. Eventually, he was put on Depakote (valporate) and Zyprexa (olanzapine).

Before each hospital discharge, he was educated about his medications and assigned an appointment for a follow-up visit. However, when the date came for that appointment, he would not show up, and attempts by the staff to contact him would be thwarted by disconnected phones or responses from landlords that he had moved and left no forwarding address.

From the time Milo had his first breakdown, I had learned to brace myself whenever I picked up the phone. Milo's actions were growing more and more bizarre. During the late 1980s, he began to write many letters to the *Reno Gazette-Journal* and other Nevada newspapers about the sinfulness of the brothels. He started an organization called Nevadans Against Prostitution.

Because of his illness, Milo could never be a responsible parent to his son Kevin, but as he became more and more zealous in all-consuming causes, his role as a father became almost non-existent. Kevin spent much more time with our parents.

September 1984

In one of my phone calls to Nevada, I learned that Milo and Kevin had moved in with Mom and Dad in Genoa.

"Yeah," Dad said, "Milo's between jobs now, and since he got kicked out of his apartment, we thought he could stay here and help me cut down some trees. It's working out fine. Today he's on the bulldozer working on the driveway."

"How's Kevin doing?" I asked.

"We enrolled him in a school in Minden." I could hear Mom in the background asking Dad who was on the phone. "(It's Cynthia.) He seems to like it."

"That's great, Dad." I felt relief that, with Mom and Dad, Kevin was in a somewhat normal situation, at least for the time being.

"Milo has an interview with a cement company in Reno tomorrow," Dad said, as if he had read my thoughts. "But he's also waiting to be called back for a job in Minden."

"That would probably be better," I said. "Minden's close to Genoa, so he could continue to live with you and save some money. Landlords want first and last month's rent and usually a deposit."

"Yeah. And that way Kevin would be with us longer." He paused. "Speaking of Kevin, it's time to go pick him up. Then we thought we'd go to that new McDonald's in Carson City."

"Well, give my love to Mom. And to Milo and Kevin. And I hope Milo gets that job in Minden."

"Keep your fingers crossed ... Bye, bye."

December 1985

At one point in his illness, Milo went through a period in which he had uncharacteristic anger. I wondered at the time if he was resentful of the all help he had received from the family. Or, I thought, perhaps he felt guilty about his illness.

Although Milo now had a job in Reno, Kevin was again living with Mom and Dad. Each morning, Kevin rode the bus from Genoa to the middle school in Minden.

During one Christmas reunion in Genoa, Milo arrived in an uncharacteristic hostile mood, and I could tell that he was getting sick again. From his remarks and behavior during that visit, I later thought about the racing thoughts that might have gone through his mind as he arrived on Christmas Eve:

They left the lights on for me...there's Cyndi and Ted's car...Teddy shoulda come by himself...Cynthia's gotten too highfalutin' lately, like I'm too strange to be her brother anymore because I live on the streets sometimes...bet she couldn't survive ten minutes by the River in Reno without her eyeliner and cashmere sweaters...Carolyn's not here yet...wish Dad had moved his truck out of the way...why doesn't HE get out of the way...Mom's O.K.... Dad should leave before I take care of him myself...wonder if Uncle Ray's coming...maybe I'll go visit him in Frisco again, take Kevin, too...Ray hasn't seen him...yes, I think I'll do that...right after dinner...I brought presents for everybody...I'll ask Mom if she's got some wrapping paper...or maybe she can wrap 'em for me, and wash my clothes too...I'll tell her I'll cook the turkey for her...I hope she made fruitcake...I hate fruitcake...I'll tease her about it...there's Blackie waiting for me...nope, I don't see Ray's Cadillac...yup, I'll go to Frisco, maybe tonight, maybe tomorrow...my boss won't care...he told me to go to hell anyway.

"Hi, Blackie. How's this old dog?"

Jeez, sure is cold...hope they got me the usual warm jacket, this one's got holes in it...but maybe I'll go to Las Vegas instead, it's warmer there...they probably have lots of construction jobs down there, even in the winter...yeah, that's what I'll do, or maybe drive to Florida...wonder if this old jalopy would make it...I hear the Florida Keys are eighty degrees this time of year...

"Knock, Knock! Ho, Ho! Merrry Christmas!"

March 1986

"Hi, Mom. How are you? How's Milo?"
"Cynthia! What a treat to hear from you during the week! Milo's still in the hospital," she answered.
"So you still have Kevin with you?" I asked.
"Yes, and it's just as well. He needs surgery for his eye—the one that still crosses. So we'll take care of that while we have him here."
"Is Dad still helping him with his reading?"

"Oh, yes. Every day we go to the library for more books and take back the ones they've read the night before."

"That's great, Mom. I'll bet Kevin's mother never read to him once."

"You know, I've learned that people with mental illness are distracted much of the time," she said. They're just 'not there' for others, and that includes their children."

"That poor kid," I said. "What kind of chance does Kevin have? Isn't there any possibility the courts will let you and Dad adopt him?"

"We thought about talking to an attorney after Milo got sick last time. But Milo is his father, and he has the right to custody of his son unless he is physically abusive or unable to provide for him. And, you know, when Milo isn't sick, he can hold down a job that pays pretty well."

"But you and Dad could take so much better care of Kevin. You could get him special help—on his speech, for instance. And his hyperactivity. Every time I tell Milo that Kevin has special needs, Milo just dismisses it and says, 'Oh, he's O.K.'"

"I know," Mom's voice was full of resignation. "But Kevin wants to be with Milo. When we ask him he always says, 'I wanna be with m'Dad.' And, of course, we're always hoping that Milo will get better."

"How can a kid Kevin's age know what is best for himself? So Milo has 'his rights!'" I spit out the words through clenched teeth. "I can't believe the world has come to this!"

"In the meantime," Mom's voice was resigned, "we'll help Milo out with Kevin whenever we can."

~~~

People with bipolar disorder can lead healthy and productive lives when the illness is effectively treated ... Without [proper] treatment, however, the natural course of bipolar disorder tends to worsen. Over time a person may suffer more frequent (more rapid-cycling) and more severe manic and depressive

episodes than those experienced when the illness first appeared.

– Goodwin FK, Jamison KR. *Manic-Depressive Illness.* New York: Oxford University Press, 1990, National Institute of Mental Health Publication "Bipolar Disorder," 2001

It's a raw, primitive feeling coming from deep inside the body. Perhaps that's why the limbic system is sometimes called the visceral brain. It feels. You can't shake the feeling. Then the "thinking" areas take over. There is an intellectual fixation on this quirk of fear in the underlying system. The fear creates a premonition, a warning of impending danger ... The paranoid becomes rigid and inflexible. He is attuned to any possible threat ... It is necessary to stand on guard against any external force or authority.
– *Whispers: The Voices of Paranoia*, by Ronald K Siegel, Simon & Schuster, 1996, ISBN 0684802856

Chapter Eighteen: The Mafia

September 1987

Dayton, Nevada, is set in sagebrush on a stretch of U.S. Highway 50, just east of Carson City. Until the population boom in the late 1990s, there was one diner/casino and not much else. Dayton's other claim to fame was its proximity to a local brothel.

It was late summer, 1989. Milo suddenly announced to Mom and Dad that he had allied himself with an ex-F.B.I. agent. He said that he was having "confidential" meetings with him at the diner in Dayton.

Milo dropped hints that he was working undercover for this agent on a special assignment. He was supposedly helping him to gather information about the shady things going on in the brothels with "The Mob." Milo would not reveal the name of this person, claiming that would be too risky.

As Milo told it, the man would wait in a booth in the back of the place, near the restrooms. Milo would take a seat at the bar, order a drink, and look in the mirror behind the bartender to see if anyone suspicious might have followed him in. Soon, he would take out a sheaf of notes from under his jacket, slip them under his arm, and casually drop them on the agent's table as he headed for the john, winking at the man as he passed by. When Milo came out again, the man would be gone.

One Sunday, Milo arrived at our parents' home with a bruise on his forehead. He claimed to have been mugged when he went to pick up his mail. He vaguely alluded to the fact that the attack had been a warning; next time it might be worse.

During that fall, none of the family heard from Milo for weeks. Mom and Dad contacted his landlord, his boss, the pastor at his church, and finally the police. He was still missing two months later.

We began to wonder if he really had met with foul play, due to his activities against the brothels, and we feared that he might be at the bottom of one of the many deserted mine shafts somewhere in Nevada. Then, in late December, Milo suddenly showed up.

It was eight o'clock on Christmas Eve. Ted and I had arrived in Genoa that afternoon. The box of See's Candy had been opened and passed around, and we were watching the bald eagle perched in the tree outside the kitchen window. It had just started to snow.

As usual, there were lists surrounding the Girl Scout calendar on the side of the refrigerator. "Bread, eggs, milk" headed the longest one. Others included what to tell the doctor, when to call the propane man, what to order from Sears. On one scrap of paper, Mom's handwriting was less sure, more halting.

When we find Milo, be sure to call:
  Ray
  Sis

Cynthia & Ted
Carolyn & the girls ...

The knock at the door was surprising; we seldom had visitors up here. The house was built on a mountain on the east side of the Sierras. It was accessible only by a steep dirt road, and it was treacherous at night or in bad weather.

"Ho, Ho, Ho! Merrrry Christmas!"

Mom and I looked at each other as Dad went to the front door. We all knew that voice as well as our own.

"Milo!" Mom hugged him. "Where have you been?"

"I had to lay low for awhile. I've been in Arizona."

"How did you get here? We didn't hear a car."

"I got a ride from Reno. They dropped me off on Genoa Lane, and I walked up."

"Why didn't you call or write?" I asked.

"They'd know. They know everything I do."

"Who's 'they?'" Dad looked alarmed.

"You should go to Phoenix sometime. Real nice there. Much warmer 'n here."

Ted had come into the room. He and Milo shook hands. "Wanna go to Elko?"

"What did you do in Arizona, Milo?"

"Worked in construction. Concrete. I think I'll move there."

"Kevin keeps asking about you," Mom said.

"How is he?"

"Fine," Dad answered. "He's asleep in the loft."

"Are you hungry, Milo?"

"No."

Later, as Mom and I made up the daybed in the living room, I noticed Milo sitting in the rocking chair by the big bay window, his glazed eyes looking out into the night.

~~~

Paranoia is a term used by mental health specialists to describe suspiciousness (or mistrust) that is either highly

exaggerated or not warranted at all ... Because many psychiatric disorders are accompanied by some paranoid features, diagnosis is sometimes difficult.

– *Useful Information On ...Paranoia*, revised by Margaret Strock, Office of Scientific Information, National Institute of Mental Health, July 14, 2005

Part Five:

Tilting at Windmills

The Anti-Brothel Crusade

The charging of his enemy was but the work of the moment.

– *Don Quixote de la Mancha,* Miguel de Cervantes

Increased *self-esteem* is [a] major manifestation of mania ... If the mania progresses, the person's increased self-esteem develops into frank grandiosity.
   – *Surviving Manic Depression*, by E. Fuller Torrey, M.D., and Michael B. Knable, D.O., Basic Books, 2002, p. 26

Chapter Nineteen: A Spiral of Zeal

In 1988, I read an article in the paper about the danger of HIV in the brothels. I then spent thousands of dollars of my money placing ads in the Reno and Las Vegas papers describing the evils of prostitution. This resulted in articles about me. I became hungry for fame. I would call reporters hoping they would print something about me. I had purpose; I felt important. I was also getting sick.

Using the name John Reese, Milo began a decade-long crusade against the brothels of Nevada. With his Paul Newman smile, innate charm, and seemingly logical arguments for his cause, he won over many conservatively religious citizens. Later, he would lose most of these supporters.

During this time, he used most of his wages as a construction worker to pay for full-page advertisements in the *Reno Gazette-Journal* imploring legal prostitutes to come forward.

"TELL NEVADANS ABOUT HELL IN THE BROTHELS," said one.

Another ad asked the sex workers to tell of sexually transmitted disease, minors in the brothels, abuse, and drugs. One asked prostitutes if they were aware of any of their colleagues working while HIV positive.

Written at the bottom of one full-page rant was this:

We are a nondenominational Christian organization campaigning to close the brothels because we love everyone involved with prostitution and because we love Jesus Christ, the author and finisher of our faith.
  – Paid for by Nevada Against Prostitution,
  John Reese, Chairperson

Milo later told Ted that he had visited the brothels himself during his first year of college at the University of Nevada in Reno. After becoming religious, he said, he started this crusade to assuage his guilt. He began to lobby legislators. He wrote more than seven hundred letters to the editors of local newspapers. Whenever the opportunity presented itself, he would give interviews to the media.

In 1993, Milo paid for two billboard ads on the highway outside the Mustang Ranch saying:

WARNING: BROTHELS ARE NOT AIDS-SAFE!

The 3M National Advertising Company covered over these billboards a short time later, fearing liability from the brothel industry. George Flint, of the Nevada Brothel Association, expressed his frustration with Reese's tactics in a letter to the *Reno Gazette-Journal* in 1992:

"John can't seem to make up his mind. One time he attacks from a religious perspective, next from a moral viewpoint. His latest effort comes from a medical tack. Regardless, he seems to be off base."

Milo tells his version of his assault on the medical tests:

In 1993, I asked the Center for Disease Control to send me a report of all brothel H.I.V tests for 1992. The Nevada

State Lab had analyzed 4,010 of a total of 4,478 of these tests. I called the C.D.C., and they would not tell me where the missing 468 tests were analyzed. They contacted Will Scott of the Nevada State Lab and told him not to discuss this issue with me. I discovered that a lab in Sparks, Nevada, had obtained an "exempt" lab license the same month the prostitutes' tests disappeared. This lab was on contract with Mustang Ranch.

From 1994 to 1996, I petitioned the Nevada State Board of Health meetings three times and rural commissioners meetings eight times to try to get them to access a list of eighteen pre-employment HIV prostitutes. The C.D.C. will not allow anyone to look at this list. At every meeting, a C.D.C. rep. was present and insisted that Nevada's brothels were HIV-free.

Over the years, in his debate with Milo, George Flint cited statistics on the vigorous testing program of legal prostitutes in Nevada. He quoted a leading Clark County Health Department officer who had said that, next to abstinence and monogamous relationships, "the safest sex anywhere is that which occurs in a Nevada licensed house of prostitution."

In a letter to the editor in response a month later, Milo claimed that some of those doing the medical inspections were unlicensed to practice medicine in the state of Nevada.

"This includes not only the health departments but the legal officers as well. I have been advised that [George] Flint was aware of this apparently illegal and highly dangerous practice." Milo's inflammatory comments remained unsubstantiated.

In 1994, Milo filed for a license to open a gay brothel near Las Vegas, claiming that a brothel would be a good place for gay men to have safe sex. Although he would not disclose who his investors were, he spread a rumor that he planned to open several more of these establishments within the next few years.

Later, some in the brothel industry admitted to being nervous. Brothels such as these would cause many citizens of Nevada to be up in arms. As a result, legislators might ban brothels altogether. However, Milo had no money for any kind of business venture, and he later admitted that he was not really serious about a gay brothel anyway. He was just trying to get publicity for his cause.

In September, 1995, Milo chained himself to a railing in front of the state offices of the Nevada Bureau of Disease Control. The day-glow pink sign he carried said, "Bureau of Disease Control Is Hiding Brothel HIV's."

Frustrated that the police refused to arrest him, due to his right to protest on state property, Milo kicked a length of chain across the sidewalk. The color photo which accompanied the article in the *Reno Gazette-Journal* showed him wearing sunglasses, a long-sleeved dress shirt, and tie, watching with intent as bolt-cutters were used on the chain around his wrist. Police officers stood waiting to lead him away.

To this day, Milo believes that the CDC is covering up test results:

I'm convinced the Feds are interested in preserving Nevada's brothels. Why, I don't know. Senator Bill O'Donnell of Las Vegas told me that if any prostitutes tested positive for H.I.V., all the brothels would immediately be shut down.

A spokesperson for the Nevada State Health Division claimed they had gone over their statistics many times and found nothing supporting claims or evidence of any missing tests. Milo told the media that his organization was concerned with more than the physical health of prostitutes in Nevada.

"We believe the Lord has a better job, a better life for all of them," said Milo.

After Milo married his second wife, Susan, he attended church regularly and held a job in construction for nearly two years. Matrimony seemed to agree with him. We thought he had settled down.

In July 1996, Milo and fellow brothel opponent George J. Williams III sued district attorneys and sheriffs in Clark, Lyon, and

Storey Counties. (Storey County housed the famous Mustang Ranch, and Clark County allowed prostitution outside of its main city, Las Vegas.) This lawsuit came after the two men had made an unsuccessful attempt to get records of prostitutes in these locations in order to study the relationship of prostitution and sexually transmitted diseases.

In August 1998, an organization called "No Brothels in Lyon County Association" had their mass mailing campaign backfire on them when many of the recipients were offended at what they called lewd photos on the flyer. One citizen threatened to sue the organization but could not find a return address on the envelope or discover who was behind the group. The organization was not registered with any state agency. Later, Milo hinted that he had had a role in this campaign.

In May 1998, Milo announced that he was going to run for Nevada state assembly. The district included southwest Reno, Incline Village, and parts of Carson City. When reporters asked him whether he would work to close the brothels if elected, he made the startling announcement that he was giving up his anti-prostitution crusade—for now. Instead, he said he would try to reduce sales and property taxes and push for a "back to basics" approach to education.

Milo lost the election, but he received 600 votes.

On November 9, 1999, the *Reno Gazette-Journal* featured a color photo on its front page showing police and search dogs beside an abandoned blue car on a sagebrush lined gravel road. The caption explained that the road was off Interstate 80 and near the Old Bridge Ranch Brothel. The car door was open, its window broken. There was blood on the seat. The driver, identified as Milo John Reese, was missing.

The police called the situation "suspicious." They were baffled as to what might have happened.

The manhunt included the use of trackers, forensic investigators, and airplanes from the Washoe County Sheriff Search and Rescue Air Squadron. Citizen volunteers searched for footprints, broken brush and other trail signs. Divers were ready to go into the icy Truckee River. At first, the Nevada Highway Patrol thought that the 1991 Mazda had been in some kind of traffic accident.

When interviewed, Milo's wife, Susan, said that "John," as she called him, had left the night before. He told her that he was going to a meeting at the Old Bridge Ranch, and that he would be home shortly. When he did not return, she assumed he had decided to go on "vacation," something that had been on his mind lately. (As a construction worker, he was off work in extremely cold weather.)

The article mentioned the fact that Milo did not talk about his anti-brothel campaign with Susan any more because it worried her. She neither knew who he was on his way to meet nor exactly why he was going to the Old Bridge Ranch. Investigators talked to people at the brothel. At first, they did not rule out the possibility that someone there was involved.

The next day, the *Gazette-Journal* printed a photo with a description of Milo John Reese: "6-foot-1, 195 pounds, brown hair and blue eyes. He was last seen wearing a navy blue sport coat, white short-sleeve shirt with a tie and black slacks." There were phone numbers to call if anyone had seen anything.

On November 18, 1999, ten days after his bloodstained car was found near Reno, Milo was photographed on videotape withdrawing money from an ATM in Sacramento. The police later picked him up in Las Vegas and put him on a plane back to Reno.

Milo admitted that he had used a rock to break the window of the car and that he had cut himself with a piece of the glass to stain the car with his own blood. He said that he had been trying to gain publicity to highlight his claim that prostitutes were leaving the legal brothels to work illegally in Las Vegas and Reno. He had gone to the Old Bridge brothel to interview one of the prostitutes about this before he disappeared.

Milo apologized for the whole incident, saying, "I'm sorry I put everybody up to this, but I thought it was the only way to do it."

In Milo's words:

In an attempt to start an investigation into the past history of H.I.V. prostitutes, I traveled five miles east to the Old Bridge Ranch Brothel and inquired about a prostitute named "Nicole," the same name of a prostitute police were looking for concerning a robbery in a Sparks hotel room.

When I entered the brothel, the madam said that Nicole was off shift, but she would be available for tricks the next day. When I went back there the next night, the madam said that Nicole had quit. I talked to several people in the front room where the girls stand to be chosen, but no one could tell me about Nicole. I also asked two cab drivers if someone could theoretically take a girl to a hotel in Reno, something illegal. They said that this was done on a regular basis.

I looked into the video cameras, so that the sheriff would later know I was there. Then, for my finale after all the trouble I had caused the brothel people in the past ten years, all I had to do was to make it look like I was fed up and had decided to end my life. I drove half a mile from the brothel, put some blood on the dash board, threw a rock in the window, walked to town and took a bus to Sacramento.

Officials were up in arms. Calling this stunt "reprehensible," Washoe County Sheriff's Lt. Doug Gist told the *Reno Gazette-Journal* that it "created a dangerous and time-consuming ordeal for our deputies." He said they would be referring the case to the district attorney for consideration of criminal charges.

"Reese's willful and premeditated actions...for the sole purpose of drawing attention to his own personal agenda placed deputies, search and rescue members and others at risk," Gist told the *Reno Gazette-Journal.* He said that some of those personnel, looking for John Reese in the rugged hills near Mustang, Nevada, had come close to stumbling into an old mine shaft.

Letters to the Editor of the *Gazette Journal* expressed outrage when Milo was not charged with a crime. They presented arguments that he had committed fraud, a punishable offense. One letter accused him of being sanctimonious in preaching against prostitution while causing taxpayers to spend money looking for him. How dare he pretend to be the victim of a crime and endanger those looking for him when the money spent in the search should go to victims of real crime!

Milo John Reese was fined the $8,761 it had cost for the search. Milo told the newspapers that he would pay. "I don't believe that's a sacrifice," he said. "If I sent out any kind of message about my cause, then it was worth it." Not long afterward, he and his wife declared bankruptcy, and the money was never collected.

In January 2000, Milo was at it yet again. He filed an initiative petition to change the law to prohibit prostitution and to impose misdemeanor penalties for any violations. He made the mistake of using a copy of the petition being circulated by the Coalition for the Protection of Marriage, and they disclaimed any connection with him. Someone also observed that if he could afford to hire a crew to gather signatures for his petition, he could well afford to pay his fine to Washoe County.

Like Don Quixote, Milo could not see the fine line between idealist causes and the reality of the world.

~~~

Common Risks:

If your mood disorder goes untreated or under-treated for too long, you risk:

   – **having your spouse or significant other get fed up and leave you**
     – **losing your children or your right to see them**
     – **having your family disown you**
     – **having your friends desert you**
     – **becoming socially isolated**
     – **missing work and getting fired**
     – **having massive financial problems**
     – **losing all of your possessions**

–becoming dependent on underfunded government assistance
– winding up in jail
– becoming homeless and living on the street

– Bipolar Disorder Demystified: Mastering the Tightrope of Manic Depression, by Lana R. Castle, Marlowe & Company, An Imprint of Avalon Publishing Group Inc., 161 William St., 16th Floor, New York, NY 10038, 2003

An unmistakable sign of paranoia is continual mistrust. People with paranoid personality disorder are constantly on their guard because they see the world as a threatening place. They tend to confirm their expectations by latching on to any speck of evidence that supports their suspicions and ignore or misinterpret any evidence to the contrary. They are ever watchful and may look around for signs of a threat.
– *Useful Information On…Paranoia*, revised by Margaret Strock, Office of Scientific Information, National Institute of Mental Health, July 14, 2005

Chapter Twenty: Big Brother and STDs

The office of the Nevada State Health Division is on a tree-lined street just behind the State Capitol in Carson City. This department is responsible for tracking all infectious diseases in the state, sexual and otherwise.

On August 27, 2003, I interviewed Dr. Randall Todd, the State Epidemiologist. I knew that Todd had been one of the targets of my brother's anti-brothel crusade.

Dr. Todd was perhaps in his mid-fifties, of medium height, and meticulously dressed. He held a notepad on which he had written down some things he wanted to tell me. Because of his long tenure in this office, he had come to know Milo well.

Todd proceeded to give me a brief history of how the state of Nevada had regulated sexually transmitted diseases (STDs) in the brothels. Until recently, he had worked with a man named Bob

Nellis, the program manager from the federal Center of Disease Control.

In the late 1980s, Todd said, there were no state laws concerning STDs. Their regulation was left to the individual counties of Nevada. However, with the advent of AIDS, it was decided that, rather than close all the brothels, clients would be required to use condoms. Legal prostitutes would be tested on a regular basis. The results of the tests would then be sent to Nevada Public Health Department and to the federal Center for Disease Control.

The prostitutes in Nevada's brothels are currently tested weekly for chlamydia and gonorrhea and monthly for syphilis and HIV.

"The thirty state brothels used to see two hundred cases of sexually transmitted diseases every year, mostly gonorrhea and syphilis," Todd said. "Last year there were twelve cases of STDs, all of them chlamydia or gonorrhea. There were no cases of syphilis or HIV.

"Although there were twenty-seven HIV positive tests since 1985," continued Todd, "these were among *applicants* to the brothels, not workers. They were not hired."

Tests were originally done by state laboratories. However, Dr. Henry Solaway, who owned Associated Labs, complained that any licensed laboratory in Nevada should be able to do the tests, even if these labs were privately run.

Dr. Todd told me that [Milo] John Reese called the Nevada Public Health Department in the early 1990s and asked how many HIV tests had been done that year.

At this time, he was given one figure; when he called back and talked to Bob Nellis, he was given another.

The discrepancy in numbers occurred because the first person had given Milo only the number of tests done at the state lab. Bob Nellis had quoted the number that included *all* tests, those done by the state and those done by private labs. However, Milo would not believe this. He then concluded that the 400 plus difference in numbers must include some HIV positives.

"Carl Primmer, who was Milo's fellow anti-brothel crusader, wrote to Donna Shalala of Health and Human Services, then to President Clinton. He demanded they see to it that Nevada release these medical records," said Dr. Todd. "He threatened to sue the Nevada Board of Health as well."

Todd told me that another member of the anti-brothel group, George Williams III, had written a novel about how the owners of the brothels had bought off the local city councils. The characters were thinly disguised with pseudonyms. It was not difficult to figure out that he was talking about Joe Conforte, owner of the Mustang Ranch, and his madam, now on the city council.

"Nevada is still a small state," Dr. Todd went on. "People have easy access to government. And the culture of that government is that you don't blow people off. You return all calls from citizens. Therefore, John got a response."

When I told Dr. Todd about Milo's bipolar illness, he said, "It fits the pattern. There was much contact at times, and then we wouldn't hear from him for months."

Dr. Todd explained how Milo had attacked the state's claim that tests declared negative might have been taken in a "window period." According to Todd, there had never been a "conversion" in which a prostitute became HIV positive during the time that elapsed from application to becoming a line worker. (The term "line" comes from the ritual of the "line-up," where clients choose a woman when they enter the brothel.)

Todd assured Milo that none of the jurisdictions had issued work permits for any of the applicants who had tested positive. "I told John," he said, "that there was no transmission of HIV in the brothels."

Milo then phoned the sheriffs and police chiefs in the different counties and asked if the Nevada Health Department reported test results to them. They said no. However, Dr. Todd contended that Milo had asked the wrong people. Test results were reported to other officials, not local law enforcement.

When Milo paid for the giant billboard beside Interstate 80 at the exit leading to the Mustang Ranch and the Old Bridge brothels, the brothel industry managed to have it removed due to a violation of a law concerning distance from the highway.

Once, Milo got on the agenda of a meeting of the Nevada Board of Health in Las Vegas. He complained that the Health Division was not telling the truth. When asked to supply proof,

Milo dumped a large envelope of tapes on the table, claiming that these were conversations he had had with prostitutes who worked in the brothels.

Someone at the meeting pointed out that there would be no way to ascertain who the people were on the tapes. Therefore, they could not be used as evidence of proof. A board member asked Milo just how many members there were in his organization, Nevadans Against Prostitution. The ads sponsored by this group had implied that there were hundreds. After hesitating, he admitted that there were only five.

Dr. Todd had been present at a city council meeting in Fallon, Nevada. They were discussing the Salt Wells brothel, which had been shut down for thirty days following an incident when two girls worked without permits. Milo was there to make a presentation.

Before they recognized him, however, one member stated that brothels were legal, that they had been voted for by the people of Nevada. And Milo would not change anyone's mind about this.

When Milo was called upon, he said that the woman sitting next to him was his attorney, and he would like for her to make a statement. This was not allowed, as she was not on the agenda. It was decided that the Salt Wells brothel would be reopened.

Speaking about Milo's personality, Dr. Todd said, "Even though he and I were adversaries, he always greeted me like a long-time friend. When I saw him at those meetings, he would say, 'Hi, how are you? How was your trip down here?' Things like that. During those encounters, John was affable and pleasant."

Pahrump, Nevada, where prostitution is legal, hosts the Chicken Ranch brothel. When Dr. Todd was asked to attend a meeting in Pahrump (just northwest of Las Vegas), in order to present data, Milo was also there. Milo went through his usual presentation, giving reasons why Nevada's brothels should be closed down.

Todd then shared his information about legalized brothel HIV testing. He compared its good record to that of Las Vegas, which does not have legalized prostitution. Todd told the group that approximately three hundred cases of HIV among illegal prostitutes are reported each year in Las Vegas, and fifty of them constitute a second offense. This is a felony, according to law.

Addressing Milo, one member of the council then said, "It seems that we have it good here. Why don't you go to Las Vegas and fix *that* problem? Then come back and talk to us."

Dr. Todd had tried to talk Milo about this many times. If Milo wanted to do something about prostitution and sexually transmitted disease, he should start with *illegal* prostitution. But Milo did not seem interested in that.

As his crusade went on, Milo's letters to the newspapers became increasingly more animated. Dr. Todd said, "I told him, 'John, you don't tell the truth in these letters!' He then sent me a letter of apology."

Todd rose from his chair, walked to the window, and pointed down at the entrance below. "John chained himself to that railing out there two or three times. On one occasion, he used a bullhorn and yelled, 'Dr. Todd, come down here and face the charges! The Nevada Health Division is hiding tests!'

"After the police refused to arrest him," Todd said, "he tripped a blind man who was on his way into the building. This time, the cops obliged."

Another time, Milo rented a late-model Cadillac, taped signs all over it, chained himself once more, and stood on the car yelling his accusations. He had brought what he thought was enough money to make bail, but after being arrested this time, the stakes were raised and he could not pay. Todd assumed that he had spent that night in jail.

At some point, in a complete about-face, Milo suddenly conceded that the state's HIV testing *was* effective. It was then he announced that he had decided to open a gay brothel in Pahrump, Nevada. This made the Nevada newspapers and provoked inquiries from out-of-state newspapers such as the *San Francisco Chronicle*.

Milo later admitted that he had never completed the application to open a gay brothel, but that was after this had received all the attention. "The brothel industry likes quiet," Dr. Todd went on to say. "They shy away from publicity."

Dr. Todd wondered if opening a gay brothel would tweak the health regulations.

"The condom part would be easy," he chuckled, "but what would we do about cervical specimens?"

~~~

In its extreme forms, paranoia slides into the realm of delusion. Many people with bipolar disorders experience less severe forms of paranoia because of personalizing events, catastrophizing, or making leaps in logic.
　– *Adult Bipolar Disorders: Understanding Your Diagnosis & Getting Help*, by Mitzi Waltz, O'Reilly Media, Inc, 2002, p. 261

Grandiosity is the exaggerated belief or claim of one's importance or identity ... In mild paranoia, grandiosity is reflected in a personal feeling of uniqueness or a condescending attitude. In severe cases, the person may believe he is perfect, universally admired, a special agent of God, or perhaps even God.
– *Whispers: The Voices of Paranoia*, by Ronald K Siegel, Simon & Schuster, 1996, p. 10

Chapter Twenty-One: The Wages of Sin

During that same trip to Reno, in August 2003, I interviewed George Flint. Although he was the Executive Director of the Nevada Brothel Association, he also had other business interests.

We had agreed to meet in Flint's plush basement office in his Chapel of the Bells, a tiny Victorian-style building complete with spire and harlequin windows. The sign outside read: "World Famous Wedding Chapel, Since 1962."

The comfortable waiting room was ornamented with vintage artwork and photography of the Old West. Items available for purchase were displayed in a large glass case. These included champagne glasses with matching imprints of lipstick, silk ring pillows embroidered with kissing doves, and scarlet-ribboned garter belts.

From a 1996 article in the *Reno Gazette-Journal*, I had learned that George Flint had grown up as the son of strict parents who were ordained ministers in the Assembly of God church. Flint himself was trained for the ministry, and he held a degree from a Bible college in Oregon. This, together with a background in photography, had led him to take advantage of Nevada's "quickie" wedding industry and open his Reno wedding chapel in the early 1960s.

To preserve his business, Flint became a lobbyist to fight against bills in the state legislature targeting wedding chapels. When AIDS came on the scene in the 1980s, Flint convinced the Nevada brothels of the necessity for the mandatory use of condoms. He agreed to become their sole lobbyist as a government relations representative.

George Flint was not what I expected. He was in his seventies, a fatherly type, and he walked with a limp as a result of a replaced hip. There were photos of his wife and family on the walls of his basement office. As he leaned back in his desk chair and looked at me through tinted eyeglasses, he talked about his childhood in a small town in Wyoming. By now we were on a first-name basis. I asked him about Milo.

"When your brother came along," George said, "the brothels were annoyed at his campaign. I was given the task of finding out why one person would be going to such extremes. Joe Conforte, who owned the Mustang Ranch, once asked me, 'What kind of *nut* would spend all that money on ads and billboards?'"

However harmless this crusader might be, the brothels were concerned that Milo John Reese represented a potential catalyst which might bring together the different factions of brothel opposition. To well-meaning clergy and proponents of family values, Milo John Reese might have been a messiah-like figure to rally their cause.

Flint told me that, on the surface, Milo came across as level-headed, but his accusations against the brothels were not factual. He changed his tactics constantly, first attacking on religious grounds, then on morality, next on female exploitation, and then on the issue of sexually transmitted diseases.

"I spent probably fifty hours trying to reason with him," George reflected.

So George followed Milo to Fallon, Ely, Las Vegas, and other places where Milo was scheduled to speak at city council or county commissioners meetings. George wanted to be there to present the side of the brothel industry and answer Milo's accusations.

"I once went down to a meeting of the State Board of Health, in Las Vegas. After John presented two or three well written paragraphs, he couldn't answer the follow-up questions. So I stood up and since I knew his arguments well by then, answered the questions for him."

The meeting ran late. On the road out of the city, George saw Milo, still dressed in suit and tie, jogging by the side of the road.

"I pulled over and asked him why he was running. He said, 'I have a plane to catch in ten minutes.' There was no way he could make that plane, but I gave him a ride to the airport to catch the next one."

Milo had indicated that he had once been a regular client at a brothel near Reno. He had given up the practice after he had had a religious experience. George presented the theory that Milo might fit into the category of guys who get emotionally involved with a particular prostitute, and, upon being rebuffed, turn against the industry.

"He was the classic example of a trick who had fallen in love," he said.

"At one time, there was the woman who had worked in a brothel in Battle Mountain whose HIV test had come back questionable," George went on. "The lady subsequently disappeared, and Milo was convinced that she'd been kidnapped. He later called me and claimed that the body had been found in Joe Conforte's garden, in Rio de Janeiro. The trouble is, Joe Conforte lives in a penthouse and doesn't have a garden.

"Another time," he continued, "Milo told me that Joe Conforte was hiding out in Virginia City, at the Cabin in the Sky (a restaurant and bar), and the feds had him surrounded. This also turned out to be false."

During our interview, George related a story about the time Milo brought a lady into the wedding chapel. He asked George to arrange their marriage.

"I'll do better than that," Flint said. "I'll pick up the whole tab! However, we'll have the wedding at the Mustang Ranch, and the bridesmaids will be the prostitutes that work there!"

Milo was not amused.

George then talked about the time Milo had obtained a job as a driver for one of the health labs doing STD tests for the brothels. He wrote to George, saying, "This will get me on the inside."

Milo subsequently lost his job for nosing into classified test results and trying to break into the lab's computers. He had also varied his route, so he could stop off at the brothels "for evidence" along the way. But he accused George Flint of getting him fired.

I asked George if there might have been any credibility to Milo's story about being mugged when he went to the post office box he used for his anti-brothel correspondence.

"My client [The Nevada Brothel Association] never did anything to strike back at John," George said. "Joe Conforte might have done something to him, if he were here, but he left before Milo did most of his campaigning against the brothels."

When Milo would demand huge amounts of material from the state agencies which they refused to provide, Milo would accuse George Flint of paying them off.

Milo was aware that George was an ordained minister, and he frequently chastised him for deserting this "most noble profession."

"John," George said, "would urge me to give up the wedding chapel and my job as lobbyist for the brothels and join with him in his campaign against them."

In all the correspondence George Flint had from Milo over the years, Milo would always sign letters to Flint with "*And remember: Jesus loves you.*"

"As time went on," George said, "John's actions became more outrageous. When he staged his disappearance in 1999, he lost all credibility."

I asked him when he had last heard from Milo.

"I must have received fifty letters from John during the past ten years," George answered. "He sent me two or three in the summer of 2001, from Florida. He told me that he was taking flying lessons, delivering pizza, and living in his car. But there was no mention of Cuba.

"One of the last letters I received from John, sent from the Florida Keys, said that he had become disillusioned with his church, and that the people had turned against him."

In a phone call from Florida a month before Milo flew to Cuba, Milo told Flint that he had one last chance to spill his guts.

"Tell us how to find Joe Conforte. Otherwise," he said. "We'll come after *you*."

"I'll be interested to know if you hear from him again," I said.

George Flint cocked his head to one side and said, "I wouldn't be surprised if John called me from the moon!"

~~~

Because of the person's often high esteem during [mania] ... there will be a tendency to continue putting effort into plans even when others reject and try to dissuade the person from engaging in them.

– Coping with Bipolar Disorder: A Guide to Living with Manic Depression, by Steven Jones, Peter Hayward, Dominic Lam, Oneworld Publications, 2002, p. 4

For some, however, this heightened self-esteem [of mania] becomes superiority. Highly manic people can become grandiose and believe God has chosen them for a special mission ...
   – *Bipolar Disorder Demystified: Mastering the Tightrope of Manic Depression*, by Lana R. Castle, Marlowe & Company, New York, 2003, p. 14

Chapter Twenty-Two: Questionable Sources

Frank Mullen, Senior Reporter for the *Reno Gazette-Journal*, covered the anti-brothel crusade of Nevadans Against Prostitution during the 1990s. He agreed to give me an interview during an exceptionally busy day. We met in the lobby of the newspaper building.

"You can thank your brother for this." Mullen held up the security card he used to gain access to the news-room. "Until John came along, we never had to use passes of any kind."

While Mullen worked his way through his stack of phone messages, he let me peruse envelopes of stories which the *Reno Gazette-Journal* had written on prostitution since 1992. There were many articles about Milo John Reese.

After awhile, Mullen suggested that we get away from the distractions of the noisy newsroom. He escorted me out to the patio, where, through the next hour and five Marlboros, he talked about Milo.

"I get people in here all the time telling me who killed Kennedy. A man walks in, looking perfectly normal, and shows me photos of five-year old girls. He tells me they're pictures of him before the government grabbed him and gave him a sex-change operation, and the C.I.A. was after him because his father was Colonel Tippet, the pilot of the Enola Gay ... Crazy, crazy stuff!

"However," Mullen continued, "the thing with John was, it was obvious from day one that he was a zealot. And I get zealots in here that do have causes worth writing about. People who are pro-choice, people who are pro-life. But these people sometimes have something to say about an important issue. That's what John was. He was a zealot. He was anti-prostitution. But he actually brought up many good points."

As an example, Mullen said that John Reese had raised the question concerning why there had never been a reported case of AIDS or even HIV in a working prostitute in Nevada.

"The answer is that there probably has been," he said, as he lit another Marlboro, "but it's probably never been reported. An idiot could see it! The state of Nevada says, 'We don't have it on paper, so it never happened.'"

In 1997, I received a tip about a prostitute at the Sagebrush Ranch Brothel who knew about another legal prostitute who was H.I.V. positive. I went into her room at the brothel and asked her about it. She said she couldn't talk about it because her room was bugged. She was fired the next day. The Las Vegas Review Journal *wrote about this.*
– Milo

"Now, who reports?" Mullen went on. "The brothels themselves! So if they don't report it, it never happened. The brothels are the ones who order the tests. They pay the companies. So, at the time I looked into it (and I doubt if it's changed), the reports would come to the state from the people who were hired by the brothels."

Mullen pointed out that, in one case, at the Mustang Ranch, a nurse without a current license had taken over her doctor-husband's practice of doing the HIV tests.

"She did the tests by using the same disposable speculum over and over. And I got this from the girls that worked in the brothel. She was doing all these things that she was apparently not only incompetent to do, but she was simply going through the motions and not getting any viable results. And she was also putting the women in danger, on top of everything else."

After he complained to the Medical Board, Mullen was told that, since this woman was not a doctor, they couldn't touch her. He then went to the Nursing Board. Since her R.N. license was not up to date, they couldn't do anything about her, either.

"Nevada is schizophrenic when it comes to prostitution," he said. "It's legal in this state, so they're supposed to be regulating it, and they spend very little time doing that. When you bring things like this to their attention, they don't want to deal with it."

Mullen told me that several years ago, when he was writing articles about this subject, there had been no interest on the part of the state in following up on reported violations.

"At some point, as any logical person would know—and as John knew—you *had* to have a prostitute test positive for AIDS. But they simply did not report that. I heard from some of the girls that worked in these places that, yes, their friend was fired for that very reason."

Mullen said he tried to track down the girls who were fired, but he said they did not want to go on record as having HIV.

"There was a street prostitute who was arrested and put away for AIDS. She was a former worker at the Mustang Ranch who supposedly was fired, but there was no record of that at the state level. The Mustang Ranch probably said that if she got AIDS, she got it after she worked for them.

"John said that under-age women were hired by the brothels. I did stories that showed that very thing. That did occur at the Mustang Ranch. Yes, absolutely. And it apparently occurred at the Old Bridge Ranch as well.

"Being a zealot, John was willing to do what many zealots are willing to do. The end justified the means for him. I could not do that. John was under the impression that, because he was on a crusade, everyone was on his side if they spoke to him about it, so he would constantly confuse me with being an activist.

"I do not care if prostitution occurs in this state or not," Mullen said, "but I *do* care if the laws of this state are obeyed. I *do* care if the bureaucrats are doing their jobs, and that's the way I approach all these stories. I'm not trying to destroy the prostitution industry. But if the women are being abused, or under-age women are being hired, or if health records are not being kept properly, that's my concern.

"John never saw that point," said Mullen. "He never 'got it,' that I'm not a crusader. I'm not on his side or the brothels' side. You bring me a good story and I'll follow it up.

"Now, John had all these theories, but he very seldom had proof. He would bring me tapes where he would have sat in the bar at the Mustang Ranch with the tape recorder running in his pocket. And he would ask a girl, 'Well, where are you from?' And the girl would answer, 'Oh, I'm from …Washington.'

"And he would try to get the girls to talk. He would ask, 'How long you been working here, uh, Samantha?' She would say, 'Three years.' And he would say, 'Gee, how old are you?' 'I'm twenty.' 'So you've been working here since you were, what, eighteen?' 'Oh, no. I was seventeen when I started.' He'd try to get them to say things like that."

However, Mullen said, even when the tapes were clear, which they often were not, there was no proof of the identity of the other person talking. Therefore, they were useless as evidence.

"When I first got the call on this campaign," he continued, "it was from Carl Primmer, who was one of the triumvirate of the anti-brothel activists. He was married to a former worker at the [Mustang] Ranch.

"Carl used to manage a motel on Fourth Street [in Reno]. He was against the brothels based on the fact that his wife had gotten a raw deal when she was working for Joe Conforte. Carl knew what John knew—and I knew—that there was a lot of hanky-panky going on, especially at that time, at the Mustang Ranch.

"Women were hired without being checked," Mullen said. "They were hired without sheriff's cards. The county was very small, and a lot of the elected officials got there with the help of Joe Conforte, including his former madam, who went on to become a county commissioner. She's now doing some hard time in a federal pen. Her name was Shirley Colletti. After the IRS clamped down on Joe, she ran the ranch and then became his 'fall guy.'

"But Joe, of course, is living in Ipanema, in Brazil, sitting on the beach, smoking cigars, down there with some of his former workers, last I heard. And he's probably got some new girlfriends now."

I was curious about the time that Milo had claimed he was mugged as he went to pick up his anti-brothel mail, and he had presented lacerations when he went for medical attention.

"It could have been self-inflicted," he said. "We had another anti-brothel activist who staged a mugging and sat on broken glass. Then he drove over here to show me the 'evidence.'"

"It sounds as if he inspired my brother," I said.

"Well, this man would set up crimes and pretend to be the victim, and, as we know, John did that later with the [staged] kidnapping. So I wouldn't put it past him to do it with the mugging."

Mullen went on: "And the way Conforte and Burgess (the owner of the Old Bridge Ranch brothel) felt about John, they thought he was a gadfly who wanted attention. They considered him an annoyance but not a threat.

"With the billboards, the ads, the demands for open records, the issues John raised were one hundred percent valid. The *proof* he brought to me was either manufactured or unusable, but I always treated him with respect because I thought he was dedicated and sincere about this. He didn't go about it in a way that produced useful evidence, but, on the other hand, even a blind squirrel finds a nut once in a while.

"I would always take the time to see him and to accept whatever it was he wanted to give me. I would listen to the tape recordings, and it was a waste of time in most cases. You couldn't tell who was talking on the tape. The woman could have been his wife. It could have been anybody. But, still, the issues he raised were completely valid.

"That was what was so frustrating," Mullen went on to say. "You had things here that needed to be out in public. Were officials doing their jobs? Were the patrons of the brothels safe from venereal disease? Was the reporting that is required by law getting done?

"Were records of the workers *open* record — that one was a hell of an issue that John raised. And I agreed, because every casino worker's card is public record, every sheriff's card is public record. Why not these girls?

"Voting records are public," said Mullen. "I can go to your county and see if you are a Democrat or Republican, and I can find out when you voted, and how long you've been registered. (The public) should be able to do this with the brothels, too, and a lot of the rural sheriffs would not let you see what should be open record."

Mullen explained how he and Milo parted ways.

"Now, when I had my falling out with him several years ago, I had heard about a traffic accident out by Elko (a town in eastern Nevada) in which a young woman was killed. She had listed her place of employment, on some public record, as the Mustang Ranch. And this girl was only seventeen. Now, if she was working at the Mustang Ranch, and her true age was only seventeen, we had a problem here.

"So I backgrounded the woman and found her relatives. She was a runaway from, I believe, Washington State. She'd fallen in with a pimp who had turned her out on the streets of one of the large cities there. He'd apparently sold her to the Mustang Ranch, and she was down here working off her contract with him. Now, this [kind of thing] was what John had suspected all along. And finally, I had proof of it independently. So I knew I had to call John for a comment—he was the natural person.

"But to get a comment," Mullen lit another cigarette, "I would have to tell him what I'd found out. I knew he'd be thrilled, because I had documents to prove this. I had pictures of the girl from her mother, and I got denials from the brothels. It was a hell of a story.

"I was working on this for a piece the following Sunday. I figured that, since John was a bit hard to get a hold of, I'd better start trying to reach him right away. But I was a little worried; I didn't want to tip off all the other media in town that I'd gotten this scoop. So I called John and swore him to secrecy.

"I told him the story. He gave me the quotes: 'This is what I've been saying all along. It's not a rare, isolated case, this is the norm for these places, and if they are going to have legalized prostitution, they've got to be able to police it and stop this from happening and not have these rural sheriffs look the other way when something like this occurs.'

"I said, 'Thank you very much, John, for your intelligent, well-crafted comments. I will definitely quote you in the story. But, *please*, don't mention this to anyone.'

"Well, the very next day, every reporter in the state, every television station, every radio station knew about this case, and some of them were calling me to get leads on it. Apparently, the second he put down the phone, John started calling people."

Mullen went on. "I called him up and read him the riot act. I said, '*You son of a bitch. How could you do this?*'

"I had tried to treat him decently. Not laugh him out of the office. I just couldn't believe that he would stab me in the back like that. He had been portraying it [to the media] as *his* find, *he* had finally found proof, and so forth.

"When I finally got hold of him, he said that he'd waited until the next day, and when it wasn't in the paper, he thought I was going to cover it up. I said, 'John, I explained to you that this was a Sunday story. I was going to run it that Sunday, page one, because that's when it would get more attention. We have more circulation on that day, and so forth.

"I told him, 'You're dead to me now. Don't call me, don't give me any tips, don't show up here with any more tapes. Fool me once, shame on you; fool me twice, shame on me. You are persona non grata with me from here on out. You are banned from the newsroom, and I will not deal with you again. I don't care if you come in here with eight-by-ten glossies of Joe Conforte slitting the throat of a five-year old. I don't care.'

"That was the last time I really dealt with him, until he staged his disappearance," said Mullen. "We had to do stories on that. But that (double cross) was the last straw, because he knew exactly what he was doing. And his excuse was, 'We're all on the same side here, we're all trying to get rid of the brothels.'

"And I told him again, 'No, we're not! I'm here to report on information that relates to the public, that might help protect the public. I am not crusading to end the industry. You are. *Don't confuse me with you!*'

"But John never understood that. If you were nice to him and wrote a story, therefore you must be on his side. I would tell him over and over that I was on no one's side. I would even quote Joe Conforte and present *his* side—though I might know it was probably bull. But, out of fairness, Conforte's side needs to be in my story, as well as John's.

"I calmed down days later," Mullen said, "but John was still mad. He showed up here and wanted to fight me out in the parking lot. I said, 'You're dead to me. I can't fight a dead person. You don't exist. So go away!'

"And then he showed up three weeks later with *another* tape! He dropped it off in an envelope and waited for me out front. He would call consistently after that saying, 'I need to make this up to you, so I'll tell you …' But I'd never return his calls.

"This was his latest tip: Right before he pulled the Cuba thing, he called me from Florida and said, 'Joe Conforte is here. He's in the custody of a federal marshal. I'm telling you this because I owe you big from the time I burned you.'

"So he made me waste an entire day calling the Federal Marshal's office, the F.B.I., I called all over the country. I followed that story down because, you know, even a blind squirrel … And if Conforte really had been secretly extradited and was in some federal prison in Miami, that would have been worth reporting.

"When the Cuba thing happened, we were calling around in Florida to where John used to work, Pizza Hut, etc. I may have done one story on it, or worked with someone.

"You know," declared Mullen, "he did this just before September 11. Had it been after that, he'd probably be in Guantánamo Bay right now."

~~~

Males with bipolar disorder are more likely to get involved in potentially criminal, aggressive, assaultive, or risky behavior than females—and therefore are more likely to end up in the criminal justice system rather than in treatment.
    – *Adult Bipolar Disorders: Understanding Your Diagnosis & Getting Help*, by Mitzi Waltz, O'Reilly & Associates, 2002

From left, Cynthia Reese, age eight, Carolyn Reese, age five, Milo John Reese, age three, on the runway of their father's small airport in the San Fernando Valley.

Milo with his first bicycle, age seven, at the house on Shoup Avenue in Woodland Hills. That year, he became a Cub Scout.

During Milo's ninth-grade year, in junior high, he was voted student body president, outstanding scholar, and best athlete.

Milo branding a calf on his family's ranch in Austin, Nevada.

This photo and accompanying story was published by the Reno Gazette-Journal on October 6, 1993. Milo paid for the billboard ad with wages from his construction job. (Photo by Marilyn Newton.)

In 1995, John Reese, as he was known during his anti-brothel crusade, chained himself to this railing outside the Nevada state Bureau of Disease Control office. (Photo by Rick Gunn, Nevada Appeal.)

John Reese staged his own disappearance in 1999. Search dogs, helicopters, and law enforcement personnel spent many hours in their search. (Photo by Marilyn Newton, Reno Gazette-Journal.)

On July 31, 2001, during his solo flight in a Cessna 172 from this airport in the Florida Keys, Milo John Reese disobeyed ground instructions and headed for Cuba, where he crash-landed near Havana.

On August 9, 2001, Milo flew on a chartered jet back to the United States, where the FBI arrested him on a felony warrant for transporting the stolen plane across state borders. (Photo by Associated Press.)

M.C.S.O. Arrest Search
Results by Name
As of Sunday, June 04, 2006 at 14:06

Remember: The person or people shown on these pages have been arrested, but **have NOT been found guilty in a court of law.**
For case dispositions, and for detailed information on criminal and civil court cases, visit the Monroe County Clerk of the Courts web site.
For information on court dates and judges calendars, visit the 16th Judicial State Courts web

REESE, MILO JOHN
DoB:**11/24/1945** Age:**Unknown** Sex:**M** Race:**W**

Arrest Date: **06/03/2006** CAD #: Arrest #: **MCSO06ARR004985** Offense #: **KWPD**
Address:
GEN DEL HOMELESS, MARATHON, FL 33050
Occupation:
MCSO76MNI097919 in U.C.I. CONSULTANT
Arrest Location: **DUVAL STREET KEY WEST, 1221**
Charges:
1 Misdemeanor Count(s) of **775.13.**

Officer/Agency: **KWPD - KWPD**   Bond Amount: **$0**

In June of 2006, Milo, who had returned to Florida, was picked up on a misdemeanor charge in Key West. He was homeless at the time.

Part Six:

A Life-Long Legacy – Kevin

The gods
Visit the sins of the fathers upon the children.

– Phrixus, Euripides, 485-486 B.C.

Data from family, twin, and adoption studies unequivocally demonstrate the involvement of genetic factors in the transmission of bipolar disorder. Research to date leads to the conclusion that in most families the etiology of bipolar disorder is complex, with vulnerability being produced by the interaction of multiple genes and nongenetic factors.
– Tsuang M.T. & Faraone S.V., 1990. *The genetics of mood disorders.* Baltimore, Md.: Johns Hopkins University Press, cited in the National Institute of Mental Health *Fact Sheet on Bipolar Disorder Research*, 2004

Chapter Twenty-Three: Special Education

Milo's son, Kevin, did not know Milo as a father. Milo was the person that came and went. Without a mother, and with only his grandparents to care for him when Milo got sick, Kevin had an uneven childhood of temporary apartments, rented rooms, secondhand clothes, and cheap fast food, reflecting the long-term poverty of his father's transient employment.

The family could see that Kevin lagged behind his cousins of the same age. They read very early; he did not. They excelled in school; he struggled. They had many friends; he had none.

November 1985

There were six boys and three girls in Ruth Garner's ninth-grade special education class. The only outside light in the basement classroom came from one high window which looked out on the cement wall adjoining the stairs.

Ruth spent extra hours each day in preparing a separate and detailed learning plan for each of her students. Then, even with her teacher aide, there was the challenge of offering each student his or her own kind of specialized help.

Meeting the students' remedial academic needs was only part of her job. Most of them came from backgrounds of drug use, alcoholism, poverty, abuse, and neglect. When she met the parents, she often understood why their children had learning and behavior problems, and she was sometimes amazed that the students performed as well as they did.

Trained to notice even small changes in the behavior of her students, Ruth Garner was thrilled when those changes were positive. Progress in reading abilities, comprehension of math concepts, and success in social skills were the true payoffs in her profession.

Lately she had become concerned about Kevin. This red-haired, freckle faced boy had an infectious smile, and the sparkle in his green eyes reminded her of her older son. Even though Kevin spoke rapidly, Ruth could usually understand his sentences if she listened closely.

But these days his words were coming faster than ever. He seemed to be having a running dialogue with himself. He was more agitated than usual, and he frequently left his seat to wander around the room. This was not like Kevin, even though Ruth had a suspicion that he suffered from ADHD, attention deficit hyperactivity disorder. This was a common problem with many of her special education students.

Two days ago, Ruth had given Kevin a hall pass when she noticed his restlessness. She told him he could go out on the P.E. field for awhile, but soon afterwards, Mr. Jones, the vice-principal, brought him back.

Mr. Jones beckoned Ruth out into the hallway. He told her he had seen Kevin crossing the busy street a block from the school.

"It was weird," Jones said. "He didn't seem to look at the traffic, just plowed right across. One car slammed on its brakes. It's a wonder he wasn't killed. Let's not let him out of class again. And I think we need to call someone here."

Ruth left a message for the school psychiatrist, but so far he had not returned her call. She had listed Kevin's symptoms and asked for a complete psychiatric evaluation as soon as possible. However, she knew from past experience that Dr. Meyers had an overwhelming case load and his office was understaffed.

Kevin's behavior fit the profile of another student in Ruth's class several years before. That boy had finally been diagnosed with schizophrenia. She preferred not to think of Kevin ending up with the same fate. That student was now in his late twenties, and his family kept in touch with her. Over the years, she had learned that he had been in and out of psychiatric facilities, drug rehab, and even jail. He was now homeless.

Ruth walked over to Kevin's desk. "Would you like me to help you with your math now?" she asked.

Kevin was hunched over, his shaking fist holding a pencil. Ruth looked at the undecipherable scribbles on his notebook paper, then at his face. He was gazing out through the high basement windows, his eyes fixed at a tiny patch of blue sky.

~~~

When the illness begins before or soon after puberty, it is often characterized by a continuous, rapid-cycling, irritable, and mixed symptom state that may co-occur with disruptive behavior disorders, particularly attention deficit hyperactivity disorder (ADHD) or conduct disorder (CD), or may have features of these disorders as initial symptoms ... Unlike normal mood changes, bipolar disorder significantly impairs functioning in school, [and] with peers.

– *Fact Sheet*, Bipolar Disorder Research at the National Institute of Mental Health, February 3, 2004

The past fifty years have seen a tremendous amount of research about children with parents who have SMI [severe mental illness] ... Findings consistently point in the direction of severe stress for the children. To be a child of a parent with SMI is to have a confusing and painful childhood. Common themes do emerge... 1: The striking contrast between vulnerable and seemingly invulnerable children. 2: The enormous variation in coping strategies. 3: The extent to which social services have ignored the plight of these children.

– *The Skipping Stone: Ripple Effects of Mental Illness on The Family*, by Mona Wasow, Clinical Professor, Science & Behavior Books, Inc., Palo Alto, CA, 1995 pp. 11-12

Chapter Twenty-Four: Child Protective Services

Kevin spent several weeks in a mental hospital after getting sick during his freshman year of high school. He later described the manic months leading up to his breakdown.

"I believed I was a rock star," he said. "I would stay up night after night, listening to the music in my head."

Oddly enough, it was Milo who figured out what was wrong. Kevin was diagnosed as bipolar and given lithium. Unlike Milo, he made the decision to take his medication faithfully. In his words, he "did not want to go through the scary ride of being in a 'fast world' again."

Kevin later graduated from high school and got a job. He soon met and married someone, and they had a child. Unfortunately, like his father, Kevin chose a mate who also was mentally ill.

September 1999

"Hi, Dad. How are you?"

"I'm okay."

"Is it snowing there yet? It's supposed to rain here in Santa Barbara tonight."

"They say we'll get a foot ... but there's none yet."

"Those pine trees need it, don't they?"

"You bet they do. Hey, listen. I went to Reno today. Had lunch with Milo. Then I took him to Wal-Mart and we bought Pampers and formula for Kevin's baby. Kevin and his wife are living in a tiny little trailer."

"Must be crowded, with the baby and all."

"When I walked into that trailer, I got so depressed. I just don't know if they can do it."

"You mean be parents?"

"Yeah. Kevin takes his medication. And he works hard at the supermarket...but how much does a box boy make?"

"His wife is *really* nuts, isn't she, Dad?"

"Yeah. She talks a blue streak about nothing. Doesn't clean up, doesn't change the baby's diapers ..."

"You could call Child Protective Services."

"I know, but they would probably take the baby away. Kevin just loves that kid."

"Keep me posted, Dad."

April 2000

The Bread Board Deli was on a quiet street in Reno a few blocks off Virginia, away from the casinos and tourists. Its neighborhood was in transition. Old houses with overgrown yards were peppered with restored Victorians and brand-new duplexes.

A popular spot for lunch, the Bread Board had a variety of good sandwiches and excellent coffee. It was within walking distance from office buildings and government agencies. Today, because of the warm spring weather, tables had been set out under the awning on the sidewalk.

Mark Browne and his secretary Shirley Taylor sometimes came here for a working lunch, and they sat at one of those outdoor tables today. Here, he and Shirley could usually hold a productive meeting without the distraction of office phones.

The food came. Mark closed his briefcase, and they began to eat. "How's your sandwich?" he asked.

"Excellent." Shirley reached for her napkin and dabbed at the side of her mouth.

Mark's gaze became fixed on the sidewalk over Shirley's left shoulder. "My God, whose poor little kid is that?"

Shirley turned to see a toddler, perhaps two years old, looking up at them, his unsteady little body swaying back and forth. The boy's dirty face was striped with tears and snot. His torn pajamas were far too warm for the eighty-five degree weather. There had been a storm the day before, and his bare feet were covered with dried mud from the gutter.

Large blue eyes stared at Mark's midair sandwich.

"Are you hungry, little guy?"

"Bet he could also use a drink of water." Shirley picked up her untouched glass, stood up and held it out to the boy, who gulped while she steadied his hands.

Mark called the waitress over to the table. "Miss, do you know where this kid belongs?" he asked.

"No, but he's wandered in here before. We called the cops last time and I guess they took him home. The detective gave me a number to call if it happened again. I'll go see if I can find it."

Shirley now had the boy on her lap, cleaning his face and hands with a napkin from the empty table nearby, dipping it in what was left of the water. She started feeding him the rest of her sandwich.

"What's your name?"

The large blue eyes remained fixed on Mark.

A few moments later, a patrol car pulled up to the curb. A uniformed male police officer and a young woman with a briefcase approached the table.

"I'm Officer Platt. And this is Ms. Gray, from Children's Protective Services. Is this the little boy someone called about?"

"Yes, sir. He just wandered in here a little while ago. He seems hungry."

"And I think his diaper needs changing," Shirley pronounced, repositioning the child.

"We've taken this boy into custody before," Ms. Gray said to Officer Platt. "He lives in a trailer park a couple of blocks away."

Shirley turned to the woman. "What will happen to him?"

"Well, this time he'll probably be removed from the home and put in foster care, at least temporarily, until we can reassess the situation."

Later, as the police car pulled out from the curb, Shirley turned to Mark and asked, "What kind of parents let their two-year-old out in the streets like that?"

Mark laid down the tip while Shirley finished wiping the water stain off her skirt.

~~~

Children who have a parent with manic-depressive illness often carry the scars for a lifetime. Even when they are old enough to understand that their parent's behavior was not intentional, it doesn't always make up for the deprivation or the abuse they suffered as children.

— *A Brilliant Madness*, by Patty Duke and Gloria Hochman, Bantam Books, 1992, p. 235

For years, lithium has been the "gold standard" pharmacological treatment for bipolar disorder. When taken regularly, lithium can effectively control mania and depression in many patients and can reduce the likelihood of episode recurrence.
– Goodwin F.K. & Ghaemi S.N., 1998, Understanding Manic-Depressive Illness, *Archives of General Psychiatry*, Bipolar Disorder Research at the National Institute of Mental Health, Fact Sheet, 2004

Chapter Twenty-Five: Family Court

July 2000

The judge looked down at the slim, red-haired young man in front of him. According to the social worker's report, Kevin Reese was the father of one child, a two-year-old boy. He had a steady job as a stock worker at a local supermarket. Before that, he had graduated with a special education diploma from the Reno Board of Education. His medical records showed him to be healthy except for a bipolar condition that required daily doses of medication. He apparently complied, according to the report.

The judge noted from his other file that the woman the young man was divorcing was on state disability. She herself had a history of mental illness severe enough to impair her ability to work at any kind of steady occupation. Child Protective Services had provided a series of reports of child neglect on her part. The latest incident had caused the authorities to remove the child from her care. The woman was not in court today, nor was she represented by counsel.

The last name was familiar. Reese. Could this be John Reese's son? The anti-brothel crusader who pulled all those outrageous stunts and ran for the state assembly? The one who staged his own death and later turned up one hundred percent healthy? The judge was somehow reluctant to ask the young man who his father was.

Kevin had told the judge earlier that he was divorcing his wife because she ran up their credit cards to their limits and then spent his entire weekly wages before he could pay the bills. When asked if there were any other reasons for the divorce, the boy had seemed about to speak, then shook his head.

"Mr. Reese," said the judge, "you have requested custody of your son. I hesitate to grant this. First of all, you live in a residential hotel in a part of Reno which may not be safe for children. Secondly, you suffer from manic-depression, and although it is apparent that you take your medication faithfully, and there have been no psychotic episodes since your teen years, there is always the chance that that kind of thing could happen again. Do you see my dilemma in granting you custody?"

"Yes'r." The young man was barely understandable.

"Why do you think you could give this boy a better home than foster parents?"

"Cuz ah lov 'im. I love my son."

The judge looked into Kevin's pale green eyes for several moments, and then said, "I will grant you custody, Mr. Reese. Please don't make me regret it."

Kevin's face broke into a broad smile.

"Now," continued the judge, "here are the stipulations. You told me in chambers that you work the day shift. Is that true?"

"Tha's true."

"Your son James will be with you evenings and nights at the hotel, but I will direct that he be placed in a state-sponsored day care facility during the hours that you work. The clerk will give you a contact for that facility. Do you understand?"

"I understand."

"I also order that you place your name on a waiting list with the Reno Housing Authority. It may be several months, or even a year, but you should be able to qualify for more suitable living conditions. Is that clear?"

"Yes, sir." Kevin spoke clearly now. "Thank you, Judge!"

~~~

Parenting means being responsible for someone else's mental and physical well-being at a time when you're having enough trouble being responsible for your own. It means curbing your impulses so you can provide a little stability. It means getting out of bed to cook dinner even when depression is overwhelming you ... But parenting also means love, both given and received, and doesn't love heal?

– *Taming Bipolar Disorder*, A Psychology Today *Here to Help* book, by Lori Oliwenstein, Alpha Books, Published by the Penguin Group, 2004, p. 284

Eating properly and finding shelter from the elements is important [for everyone]—but for anyone with a serious mental illness, this isn't always as simple as it sounds. Meeting your physiological need for shelter and basic bodily safety can mean anything from taking special steps to keep your job to applying for public assistance if needed.

– *Adult Bipolar Disorders: Understanding Your Diagnosis and Getting Help*, by Mitzi Waltz, O'Reilly and Associates, 2002, p. 251

Chapter Twenty-Six: The Rancher's Inn

March 5, 2001

"Hiya, Doug."

The sign on the desk top said "Mr. Fisher," but most of the residents called him Doug. He was barrel-chested, with a neatly trimmed mustache and a long, graying ponytail. He had lost a leg in 'Nam, as he called it, and he now sat in a wheelchair much of the time despite the prosthesis he wore. After battling a drinking problem and losing his job in one of the casinos, Doug had joined Alcoholics Anonymous and Gamblers Anonymous. He now managed the Rancher's Inn, a small hotel that catered mainly to weekly guests such as truck drivers and has-been performers in the lounge acts at the local clubs.

"Doug," said the young man as he came through the front entrance. "Ahgottaprollem."

Kevin was in his late twenties, of medium height, with red hair and green eyes that crossed slightly when he was agitated. He was agitated today. He wore only a light windbreaker over a tee-shirt, although the temperature was below freezing outside. Faded jeans. No hat. No gloves.

"Rent's due today," Doug reminded him as he finished counting some bills into the drawer.

"I had the rent money in my room, Doug, and now it's gone." Kevin said the sentence as if it were one word.

"You had three hundred and fifty dollars in your room? In *cash*?" Doug asked.

Kevin slowly nodded.

Doug pushed the cash drawer in with a shove. "Why don't you ask that ex-wife of yours where the money is? She been stayin' with you again? I thought I seen her sneakin' in the back hall the other day."

"I gotta' catch the bus to pick up my boy at day care. Can you give me a few more days on the rent, Doug?"

Doug Fisher felt sorry for Kevin. The boy didn't have much to start with, and he worked hard just to scrape by and take care of his little boy. Doug thought he knew why the judge hadn't given custody to that crazy bitch, but this flophouse was no place to raise a kid. Doug tried to think of something to tell the owner, who was coming by tomorrow morning to collect the money.

"Okay," Doug said. "Till Tuesday. That's it."

~~~

The relationship between sick people and those close to them may be the quintessential case for thinking about the moral and social foundations of all human relationships. Severe illness, because it so thoroughly disrupts family life, calls attention to the taken-for-granted, normally invisible boundaries of social relationships. Prolonged illness makes demands on a child, parent, spouse, or sibling that test the relative strength of the ties that bind us together.

– From *The Burden of Sympathy: How Families Cope with Mental Illness*, by David A. Karp, copyright 2001 by Oxford University Press, Inc. Used by permission of Oxford University Press, Inc., p.15-16

If you have bipolar disorder, you can still be successful in your chosen career ... Nevertheless...people with bipolar disorder face significant challenges in the workplace. Some of these challenges arise from the stigma of bipolar disorder and the reactions of others.
      The Bipolar Disorder Survival Guide: What You and Your Family Need to Know, by David J. Miklowitz, PhD, The Guilford Press, New York/London, 2002, pp. 275-276

Chapter Twenty-Seven: Paper or Plastic?

December 24, 2002

The line was growing longer at check stand three. Marty Johnson was a fast checker, but this was 5:30 p.m. on Christmas Eve, and the other stands were even more jammed up. The situation required all hands on deck, including the part-time high school kids and the full-time special helpers.

Time-and-a-half started two hours ago, and double-time would kick in at six. Marty didn't mind; his kids would be with his ex-wife all weekend anyway. He'd have them over New Year's Day, when he'd be off. Probably take them skiing at Kirkwood.

The young man bagging for Marty had been with Rankin's for six years. He came with a special education high school diploma, and he had proved himself to be dependable and hard-working. When Kevin had started working here, Marty was one of the few who could understand what he said. The other employees had complained that he talked a blue streak, too fast to catch a word. When he asked customers what bags they preferred, his question would always come out, "Paprplas?"

But with miming and pointing, there was rarely a problem communicating. Marty had taken Kevin under his wing, always referring to his "right hand man," buying him sodas once in a while, sometimes even loaning him small amounts of money until payday. And Kevin's speech had begun to improve markedly as he had felt more capable and comfortable in his job. Customers recognized him and struck up conversations.

Marty had grown to respect Kevin. He was a model employee, never missing a day of work, during Reno's January snow or July's simmering heat. He was always well-groomed and dressed in clean clothes. Kevin had even been named Employee of the Month a couple of times. Oh, he made mistakes sometimes, like in marking prices, or in stocking an item in the wrong place. But he only needed to be told once about a mistake.

Kevin was taking on the added challenge of being a single parent. He had told Marty that he lived in a local residence hotel with his two-year old son. The little boy went to some kind of foster care during the day.

Marty had never met Kevin's ex-wife, but he'd heard about the day she had come into Rankin's to ask for money. When Kevin wouldn't give it to her, she started to beat him up, right there in the produce section. Even hurled some apples and hit him right in the nose. It took two men to get hold of her. Finally, someone called the police, and they took her away. Marty guessed that the right parent had custody of the kid.

Kevin had confided once that he had a mental illness, but that he took regular pills for it every day. He said, "I don't want to get sick like my dad."

Kevin's father was the guy who started that campaign against the whorehouses and did crazy things to call attention to himself. Everyone in Nevada had heard of John Reese. And now the whole country had, after he stole a plane and flew to Cuba.

Marty had read an article in the local paper saying that Reese was manic-depressive. If Kevin had inherited this illness, he was handling it well.

A well-dressed woman was about to pay for her two poinsettia plants and four bottles of Korbel Champagne when she remembered to ask for cigarettes. "May I have a carton of Virginia Slims Menthol Ultra Lights, please?"

"Kevin, would you get that for her please?" Marty handed over the key to the cigarette display case.

"Sure. Virginia Slims Menthol Ultra Lights," Kevin repeated.

While Kevin was gone, the woman said, "I've noticed that young man before. I could never understand him before, but he seems to talk very well now."

Marty smiled. "Yes, he's improved a lot."

December 30, 2002

Ted and I had come to Reno for the holidays, and we'd decided to surprise Kevin at work. It had just started to snow as we pulled into the parking lot.

We wandered the aisles looking for him. Finally, the manager, a short, friendly man in a black vest and tie, used his pager. Kevin was on his break upstairs.

I had not seen my nephew in several years. There came a tall, slim, handsome red-haired man in a red-orange shirt with an oval Rankin's logo above the pocket. After giving him hugs, we asked how much time he had. Could we take him out for a meal?

"I only got another twenty-five minutes." Kevin checked the large clock above the dairy section. So we agreed on something from the Rankin's Bakery instead. Donuts with sprinkles and a Coke for Kevin, decaf coffee for Ted, the real stuff for me. We found a vacant table in the enclosed mini-mall next door. Pulling up plastic chairs, we sat down to catch up on his life in the time we had.

"We're proud of you," I said, as I watched Kevin gulp down his second donut. "You've had this job at Rankin's for how long? Ten years?"

"Ten years last month. They gave me an award. And a fifty-dollar bonus."

"You take your meds every day, don't you, Kevin?" Ted leaned in over his coffee cup.

"Yeah. I don't wanna get sick again. A couple a times was enough."

"You were pretty young," I observed, "when you had your first episode, weren't you, Kevin?"

"First year of high school. But then they gave me lithium. I been takin' it since."

"You really are looking great," I said, as I smiled into Kevin's green eyes.

"Thanks." He smiled back. "I try to eat well. But ever' once in a while I have my dad bring me a pizza."

"So. You have a son, now," Ted declared.

"Yeah." Kevin's face beamed. "Three years old."

"Already? Seems like we just heard he was born! That's amazing. Your grandfather says he's a cute little guy."

"He's pretty cute, yes."

"So you take him to day care when you're at work?" I asked.

"Except when I have to work after five. Then Thomas comes over."

Thomas is Kevin's half-brother. Milo and his first wife met when they were both patients at the mental hospital in the town of Sparks, just north of Reno. Her son Thomas was three years old when they were married, and later, Milo adopted him.

"How is Thomas doing? He lives in an apartment by himself now, right? Wasn't he in a half-way house before?"

"Yeah. He got a Section Eight place. And he has a part-time job."

"No kidding. What does he do?"

"He works in a warehouse. Sorts things."

"Well, good for him! He must be taking his medication, too."

"I'm hopin' to get an apartment myself," Kevin said. "I'm on the list. Maybe February, they told me."

"That's Housing Authority too, right? You live in a hotel now?"

"The Rancher's Inn. They have rooms by the week."

"How about Amber? You two are divorced now, right? Where does she live?"

"With her mom. Sometimes she leaves, though. Her mom has too many rules."

"Where does she go when she leaves?" I asked.

"She stays with us, Thomas or me. We can't turn her out on the street."

Ted handed Kevin some money. "This is for Jimmy. For whatever he needs."

And don't let Amber get her hands on it, I thought to myself.

"Jeez, I gotta get back to work. Thanks for the donuts. And the money."

As we sought out our mud-spattered Explorer, we noticed Kevin, now wearing his Rankin's slicker, collecting grocery carts and heading toward the front entrance to the store. We waved to him on our way out of the parking lot. He grinned and waved back.

~~~

Independent people are far better equipped for life than those who are dependent on others. But, not all dependence is unhealthy. A healthy independence involves knowing when to allow for a healthy dependence, that is, interdependence ... Independent people know how to ask for help, without being influenced into blindly following someone else.

– From *New Hope for People with Bipolar Disorder*, by Jan Fawcett, M.D., Bernard Golden, Ph.D., Nancy Rosenfeld, copyright 2000 by Jan Fawcett, Bernard Golden, and Nancy Rosenfeld. Used by permission of Prima Publishing, a division of Random House, Inc.

Part Seven:

Preface to a Crime

The worst of madmen is a saint run mad.
— Alexander Pope

Freud thought that depression resulted when a person was unable to grieve adequately. Depressed people cannot allow themselves to express sadness because it's too painful. They are afraid of being destroyed by the intensity of their feelings. Instead, they avoid the grief by distracting themselves ... Someone who cannot grieve cannot accept the changes, but clings to the past with rage and anger.

– *Depression and Bipolar Disorders,* by Virginia Edwards, Your Personal Health Series, Firefly Books, Inc., 2002, p. 31. Reprinted with permission of Key Porter Books. Copyright © by Virginia Edwards

Chapter Twenty-Eight: The Funeral

Genoa, Nevada, September 1996

The old Cadillac limousine came up the steep dirt road at precisely ten o'clock that morning. We stood watching at the window as it slowly rocked its bulky body forward and back, finally facing downward on the hill. The driver opened the door, and I realized that it was the same smiling minister who had paid us a visit the day before in order to plan the ceremony.

Dad had insisted that only the three children and he ride in the limousine. Carolyn's daughters would come in their own car, while Aunt Katherine would ride with Ted in his Ford Explorer. The other relatives were to meet us at the cemetery.

But Dad did not want Milo's family there. He said, "I've had enough of crazy people."

I was taken aback by this, but I didn't see it as a harbinger of the strange behaviors Dad would demonstrate during the next few months. At the time, I read it as just another one of his eccentricities. In the months to come, I would realize it as the madness of grief.

Mom, with her unending sense of fairness, had always tried to include Kevin and his half-brother in family gatherings. I wondered if Dad had resented this reminder that there was a family legacy of mental illness.

Milo came out of Dad's bedroom, handsome in a borrowed sport coat and thrift store slacks. He wore the white shirt I'd bought for him the day before at Penney's in Carson City. His shoes were scuffed, but otherwise he looked like the middle-aged professional he might have become if things had been different.

As we pulled up to the cemetery, I could see our cousin helping Uncle Ray out of a rented Lincoln. There were other relatives in a cluster beside the arrangement of chairs facing the gravesite. Even though the casket was closed, I suddenly wished I had bought new clothes for Mom instead of the white pants and flowered blouse I had found in her closet.

The minister/chauffeur held the door open, and we trudged across the gravel to the arrangement of chairs beside the gravesite. I saw the lady from the mortuary handing out programs. Again today, she wore too much makeup, and I caught a whiff of too much perfume. She had charmed Dad into paying for "finishing touches" such as an album for the family and tarnish-resistant brass handles on the casket. He had uncharacteristically written out a check for the whopping total without so much as a "Why do we need those?"

When Dad had asked about a non-denominational minister, she had said, "Oh, yes, I know just the one!" I later wondered if this "minister" had a whole wardrobe of vestments in his closet in order to be ready for any kind of religious funeral ceremony.

It had come as a shock to me that rural cemeteries in Nevada had no grass. I imagined that our Southern California relatives were surprised as well. But the gravel was well-tended, neatly raked around the various-sized tombstones. Gravel meant there was no need to limit these monuments to flat slabs; there was no need to mow a surrounding lawn.

We embraced aunts, uncles, cousins. Everyone took seats, immediate family in the front row, facing the gaping hole of the grave beside the flower-draped coffin. Dad's brother and sister, now in their nineties, had come from Los Angeles.

It occurred to me that Mom would have liked the weather today, a cool seventy degrees. The clear view of the nearby Sierras was framed by an ultramarine sky. The changing green-gold leaves in a nearby grove of aspen trees shimmered in a light breeze.

The hot summers of the Carson Valley had been Mom's nemesis. When the heat got to be unbearable, Mom, Dad, and Aunt Katherine would go to the Nugget Casino in Carson City for the day. Mom usually beat the house at the poker machine.

After the minister read the typewritten page we had given him, he offered the opportunity for those in the audience to speak. I had written out some notes ahead of time just to have something to hold in my hands. Making a concentrated effort to focus on every word, I read about Mom's pioneer spirit, her willingness to try new ventures such as ranching and writing a political column for *The Reno Gazette-Journal*.

Others spoke of our mother's ability to make each child and relative feel special. My nieces told amusing anecdotes about their grandmother's sense of fairness. If one of their Christmas gifts cost more than the other's, the second girl would receive an envelope with the exact difference in cash. To the penny.

I noticed Ted's hands grasping Milo's shoulders from behind as Milo racked out a few words. He ended with, "I'm going to miss you, Mom."

During our vigil at the hospital, Milo had faithfully chauffeured us back and forth from the house to town. He'd been willing to pick up groceries or run errands whenever we asked.

He'd offered to sit at Mom's bedside so the rest of us could get something to eat or take much-needed naps. And he had gone on successive walks with Carolyn, then with me, in the crisp September air.

Sitting in the dining room of the Genoa house the day after the funeral, I asked Milo, who was not married at the time, if he would move in here for a few months to look after Dad and Aunt Kat. He readily agreed. He was between jobs again, and this would save on rent.

"They took care of me," he nodded. "Guess I can help take care of them now."

I told Dad about this later. He closed his eyes and slowly shook his head back and forth.

"If there's one thing I've learned over the past forty years, it's that you can't ever believe anything Milo says." He brought his right hand down on the couch pillow next to him as he said, "He means well. But he always tells people what he thinks they want to hear. After that, he might come through or he might not."

A week after I returned to Santa Barbara, I received a brief note from Milo:

Cynthia and Ted,
 I'm leaving Nevada.
Love, Milo

Dad had called it right. It was then that I realized just how little I understood my brother and his manic depression. He seemed to be that teenage brother of long ago. But that was just it. He had not grown beyond that point in his life. My concepts of "sick" and "well" now slid over each other. I was overwhelmed by the fact that this disease continued to control Milo, and indeed, would reverberate through the family for many years to come.

~~~

Any traumatic episode can trigger symptoms in people with bipolar disorder, which likely appear over-reactive to others ... Trauma produces an uncontrollable emotional upheaval, unwittingly leading to poor judgment and intrusiveness.
— From *New Hope for People with Bipolar Disorder*, by Jan Fawcett, M.D., Bernard Golden, Ph.D., Nancy Rosenfeld, copyright 2000 by Jan Fawcett, Bernard Golden, and Nancy Rosenfeld. Used by permission of Prima Publishing, a division of Random House, Inc.

Mania is the seductress of mental disorders, the psychiatric Siren calling to the passing Ulysses of the world, encouraging them to put away their lithium and enjoy, enjoy, enjoy. The Siren, however, does not tell them that the price they pay may be disaster or even death.
– S*urviving Manic Depression*, by E. Fuller Torrey, M.D., and Michael B. Knable, D.O., Basic Books, 2002, p. 263

Chapter Twenty-Nine: The Siren of Mania

April 1997

"Hi! You guys weren't due here 'till six! How did you make five hundred miles in one morning?"

Dad stood at the front door with his dog Blackie.

"We left Reno yesterday. Camped in a rest area above Mojave."

"Why not a motel? Isn't it pretty cold to camp?"

"Oh, we like the great outdoors. It was Milo's idea."

"Hi, Sis." My brother Milo walked toward me from the car. He was still handsome, but his manic-depressive illness – and hard life – had taken its toll on his tanned face, and he looked all of his fifty-five years. I noted for the first time that his hair had started to recede, and gray wove itself into his sideburns. But his six-foot body was still fit. He managed, as usual, to look stylish in second-hand thrift store clothes and worn tennis shoes.

"Sorry. Blackie will have to stay outside." I said. "And Santa Barbara has a leash law, so you may have to leave her in the car."

"Oh, she won't stray," Dad said. "Can I get some water for her?"

"Do you guys want something to drink, too? I have your beds made up."

As they sat at the counter watching me arrange pineapple and cloves on the ham, Milo boasted, "We stopped at every airport on the way down."

"Why?" *A stupid question*, I thought. *'Why' is not the operative word here!*

As if in answer, Dad said, "That was also Milo's idea."

I joined in the fun. "Let's see. You probably visited the great international airports of Minden, Mammoth Lakes, Bishop, and don't forget Mojave! Actually, Mojave's where they store those old jet planes, isn't it? What did you do at all those airports?"

"We inquired about flying lessons," Milo answered.

"Bet flying lessons are expensive, even in Mojave," I bit my tongue before I let myself ask how a day laborer could afford them.

"Lots more than Dad used to charge. Average price is about a hundred-fifty an hour. Too bad Dad let his instructor's license expire. We could rent a plane and he could teach me."

"*I* couldn't afford to rent an airplane," I said, as I took a heat-and-eat pie out of the oven. "Let alone take lessons in one."

Milo stared out the window. "You could," he stated, "if you really wanted to fly."

Milo ate little at dinner. He claimed he'd had a big lunch at McDonald's.

As we lingered over apple pie, he urged Dad to tell a flying story.

"Well, let's see. There was the time a guy was looking for someone to scatter his father's ashes at sea," Dad said. "Finally a friend of mine who knew I had a flying business told him, 'Call Oscar Reese. He'll do it.'

"So the guy called me, and we agreed on a price. I had no idea then whether it was against the law or not. It might be now, I think, but that was back in 1952. I didn't even think about it.

"So that next day, we took off – this guy, his brother, the urn, and myself, in the four-place Stinson. I gave instructions that they were to wait for me to give them a signal before they did anything. I wanted to slow the airspeed beforehand as much as possible."

"I think I know what's coming," Ted said, winking at me.

"We got out over the ocean somewhere off Malibu, and all of a sudden one of them opened the window and stuck out the urn, upside down. The debris swirled around and came right back inside the plane, all over everyone. I was cleaning ashes out of the seats for months."

Although he laughed along with the rest of us, Milo's eyes were now somewhere else, far from the reality of the moment.

~~~

"Mixed" State: Symptoms of mania and depression are present at the same time. The symptom picture frequently includes agitation, trouble sleeping, significant change in appetite, psychosis, and suicidal thinking. Depressed mood accompanies manic activation.

– *Going To Extremes: Bipolar Disorder, A brief overview,* National Institute of Mental Health website, 2001 http://www.nimh.nih.gov/publicat/manic.cfm

During manic episodes, people with this form of the illness do outrageous, outlandish things ... They feel invincible, see no consequences for their behavior, and, in fact, believe they can conquer the world. Sometimes they are certain they are God and have been entrusted with a special mission.
  – *A Brilliant Madness*, by Patty Duke and Gloria Hochman, Bantam Books, 1992, p. 29

Chapter Thirty: More Adventures of Madness

January 20, 1998

"Hi, Dad. How's your cold?"
"Oh, I'm on the tail end of it now."
"Good. Your voice sounds much better. How's the weather?"
"Sun's out today, but there's still a foot of snow and it's pretty cold."
"Can you get out if you need to?"
"I got the bulldozer running this morning. Started to clear the road."
"Well, don't overdo it out there, Dad."
"I saw Milo Sunday. I could hardly understand him, he was talking so fast."

"Mmm. Guess he's still high."

"Yeah. I asked him why he's not taking his pills, and he said that Jesus Christ told him not to."

"Oh, boy ..."

"I told him that if he took his medication, it would prevent him from doing things like just taking off for parts unknown, and he said 'Oh, those are just *vacations.*'"

"Really. Most people plan their vacations well ahead of time. Make reservations. Save up money. Pay their bills first. Take their families with them."

"Well, I guess there's nothing we can do."

"That's right, Dad. You can only take care of yourself, and *your* health."

"That's true. I appreciate your call, Cynthia."

"Talk to you soon, Dad."

Dad seemed to be handling his grief over Mom's death a bit better now, but, as I could hear in his voice, it was harder than ever for him to accept the ever-recurring burden of Milo's illness.

Milo took several trips to Florida over the next few years. Each was inspired by a manic episode. He later described what he did during these "vacations."

In 1998, I received my union vacation check of $3,700 and put $3,000 in the bank. I kept $700 in cash, and I purchased a one-way airline ticket to Florida. I reached Fort Lauderdale International Airport late on November 22 and walked to a Hollywood [Florida] *motel, five miles away.*

While in Hollywood, I took some flying lessons at the North Perry Airport in Pembroke Pines. Then I got on a bus to Key West. There was no flight instruction at the Key West Airport, so I rode the bus back up to Marathon. There, I took two lessons.

During other manic episodes, I walked a lot. On my second trip to Florida, I walked from Marathon to downtown Miami—I think it's about ninety miles—only stopping once to rest for two hours on the way. I remember a car coming close and hitting my hand with its rear view mirror. The mirror broke off, but my hand was unhurt.

During my episodes, I always experience a high level of energy and I don't require much sleep. Also, it seems, I am fearless. I am not afraid to sleep in the woods. I have no concern for any person robbing me, or for snakes or other predators.

During each of these trips, Milo called home after the mania wore off and the inevitable depression set in. Again, someone sent money and a plane ticket back home.

On New Year's Day of 2000, I called him in Reno. As in many previous conversations, Milo proved to be the "Artful Dodger."

"Hi, Milo," I said. "Glad you're home!"

"Good to be back. Where are you?"

"Oh, I'm calling from Santa Barbara."

"Thought you might be here in Reno. Maybe a New Year's ski vacation. Lots of new snow in the mountains."

"Have you seen a doctor?"

"Yeah. Boy, Florida was great. Have you ever been to the Keys?"

"No. Did the doctor give you new medication?"

"Yeah. Say, we gave Dad some Christmas presents to send you."

"What kind of medication?"

"I don't know the name. Hey, how's Teddy?"

"He's fine. Will you promise me you'll be taking your meds every day? You really don't want to go through this again, do you?"

"No. Can I talk to him?"

"You were living on the street, weren't you?"

"Motels, till my money ran out. Have you ever flown stand-by?"

"How does Susan feel about your leaving? Isn't she upset with you?"

"No. Lemme talk to Ted."

"He's gone out to breakfast with a friend."

"How's your cat George? We have three cats. They're taking over the place."

"What else did the doctor say?"

"Here's Susie. Say 'hi' to her. Bye."

After I had a brief conversation with Milo's wife, I hung up the phone feeling frustrated but somewhat impressed at Milo's ability to skirt around my questions. Sick he might be, dumb he was not.

One night soon after this, Dad called me. I pictured him sitting in the rocker in the living room, looking out over the Carson Valley in the early winter dusk, as lights came on down below in Genoa.

"Hello."

"Hi, Dad."

"Wow. Thanks for the Valentine card, Cynthia."

"Did you and Blackie go to Wal-Mart to celebrate?"

"Yeah, we went and bought a big bag of dog food for seven dollars."

"How's Milo?"

"Well, I'm looking around for a used car for him."

"Oh?"

"He got his old job back, delivering pizza, you know, and he needs a car."

"Don't you think he should …?"

"I'll find something. Milo's pretty good at fixing up old cars when they break down."

"He's pretty good at breaking them down, too. How's the weather up there?"

"No snow, but real cold. I bought Milo a new jacket. You know, he'll be outside a lot on this job of his."

There was still that persistence in his voice, the hope that at last, this time, things might work out for Milo.

"Well, I'll call again soon. You stay warm, Dad."

That next fall, Milo suddenly went to Florida again, but this time he convinced his wife, her daughter, his son Kevin, and Kevin's wife to go with him. On November 15, 1999, Milo sent us a letter from Miami on Hyatt stationary:

Ted & cyndi,

> we Moved to miami
> can't make it back to Nevada for Xmas ...
> will mail Presents.
> please firgive me for calling Cynthia a whore because she wore false eyelashes back in the 60's
> this Was uncalled for and I Deserve to Have my Lights Punched out
> wanna go to Elko?
> Love Milo

I suspected that he was sick once again. His all but illegible writing, poor spelling and lack of punctuation gave me the usual sure sign. And later, while reading about bipolar disorder, I learned that inappropriate guilt is one of the manifestations of this illness.

Milo and his family soon moved back to Reno, broke and discouraged about not being able to find jobs in Florida. Once again, Milo was delivering pizza, and Kevin was back at the supermarket.

Every once in a while we would see a glimpse of responsibility in Milo. It was as if he came up for lucid air between episodes of madness. At these times, his conscience functioned as it was supposed to, in the world of reality. In March of 2001, Ted and I received one of his more clear-headed letters:

> *Dear Ted & Cyndi—*
> *Hope you two are doing well. Kevin's baby is healthy and getting bigger every day.*
> *Dad is doing great. We see him about every other week. I'm just a little concerned about him because he's alone now.*
> *Do you have any suggestions as to my role in this as far as changing Dad's living arrangement?*
> *Or since everything is fine now with Dad, should I leave well enough alone?*
> *Love, Milo*
> *P.S. We're planning a Birthday Party for Dad after I get my next paycheck.*

In the U.S., a large percentage of homeless people have a major mental illness. Many others coping with mental illness are just one paycheck away from losing their homes. The stress that comes with living on the edge financially can actually cause [bipolar] symptoms to worsen.
 — *Adult Bipolar Disorders: Understanding Your Diagnosis and Getting Help*, by Mitzi Waltz, O'Reilly & Associates, 2002, p. 252

There is no mincing words about it: Medication does take away the high periods…moods are more stable … *But stability also means giving up the intensity of the roller coaster ride that bipolar disorder provides.* **In other words, taking medication can mean increased stability at the cost of the exciting…features of the disorder.**
     – *The Bipolar Disorder Survival Guide*, by David J. Miklowitz, PhD, Guilford Press, New York / London, 2002, p. 135

Chapter Thirty-One: Return to the Callahan

May 2001

The old Ford pickup wound its way slowly up the dirt road along the lower meadow. Alfalfa had long since gone to seed, replaced by wild meadow hay, now waving with sensual rhythm in the noonday sun. There it was, the tin-roofed house, its size dwarfed by familiar poplars, their wire-gray branches just beginning to show a spray of yellow-green.

The barn was no longer there. The present owner had bought this place mainly for its water from the two springs up in the main canyon, and cow horses were no longer needed on the Callahan. Now he owned most of the valley and ran thousands of cattle.

"Mr. Inshospe was sure glad to see us." Milo had been talking constantly since they left Reno at five this morning. It was now eleven o'clock. They had gone to visit the Inshospe ranch first, to get permission to stay here a few days.

"There he was on the tractor, still doing a lot of the chores himself, at least at his main ranch. He sure looks fit for seventy-six," Dad said.

"Ya know, Dad, we haven't been on a trip together since we all went camping at Lake Huntington that time."

"I remember. How old were you? Ten? Eleven? When was that? Nineteen fifty-five? Fifty-six?"

"I must have been twelve, because we had that fifty-six Ford station wagon."

"You're right. We have pictures of that trip, the three of you leaning against it."

"Remember, they had just found that World War II fighter plane at the bottom of the lake? With the pilot still inside?"

"Oh, yes. I'd forgotten about that."

As they slammed the doors to the truck, they noticed the old baler sitting out by the barbed wire fence. Even with its wheels and peripheral parts removed, there was no mistaking its familiar, boxy hulk.

"How many bales you think we put up, Dad?" Milo assumed a characteristic pose, his weight on one leg, arms folded across his chest. He looked around.

"Well, eight years we were here. Times forty to sixty tons or so per summer. Let's see, each bale weighs about eighty pounds…"

"What did they do with the old John Deere?" Milo wondered. "We could fix it up and donate it to a museum. What year was it made?"

"Probably in the late thirties, early forties," Oscar guessed. "So it would have been twenty years old when we bought this place. But, you know, it ran better than any other vehicle we had."

They walked around the house. The old, rusty triangle was still hanging from a branch of the aspen tree near the back porch by the stream.

"Remember all those times Mom would call us for dinner with this?" Milo reminisced. "We could even hear it down by the bottom fence."

"Yeah. Did you bring your pills, son?"

"Naw. Don't need 'em right now."

Milo stared down the valley, then turned and walked toward the house. The thick, wooden front door made its familiar squeak as Milo slowly pushed it open. Mr. Inshospe had said it would be unlocked. The place hadn't been occupied since the ranch hand living there had moved to town last fall.

The kitchen table was covered with dead insects, the floor littered with rodent droppings. Oscar entered, looked into the next room, hoping to find a broom.

"These stone walls are two feet thick," said Milo. "They sure kept in the heat in the winter, didn't they?"

"And they kept the heat *out* in the summer." Oscar wiped off the table with his hankerchief and set down the cooler and thermos. "Want a sandwich, Milo?"

"No. Not hungry."

Milo had eaten little breakfast when they stopped at that diner in Dayton, one hundred fifty miles ago. His loss of appetite was a warning sign.

Oscar opened the cooler and unwrapped a peanut butter and jelly sandwich made at five that morning.

"Maybe we can catch some trout for dinner," he said. "I brought my pole."

In response, Milo stared through the window, out toward the lower meadow. "I think I'll move to Florida."

Oscar's fitful sleep was broken by what sounded like a screaming woman. A mountain lion was prowling not far away. He eased out of his sleeping bag and climbed out from the bed of the truck. The thought of mice running over him in the middle of the night had kept him from sleeping inside the house.

Grasping the .22 rifle from the rack of the cab, he crept toward the house. The temperature had dropped dramatically during the night; clouds had covered the moon. The weather report yesterday had predicted that central Nevada could get a late spring storm this week.

Last night Milo had announced that he was going to sleep in his old room. He had thrown his sleeping bag on an old mattress in there.

"Milo, you hear that?" Oscar called as he opened the front door.

No answer. When he looked into the back bedroom, he could see that Milo's sleeping bag was empty.

At dawn, Oscar was still sitting in the old rocker by the smudged dining room window. His doze was broken by the slam of the screen door.

"Milo?"

"Yeah." Milo's voice was flat. He did not say where he'd been.

"Shall we pack up and go?" Oscar asked. "Have some breakfast in town?"

Milo did not respond but gazed out the window to a point only he could see on the distant hills.

"Yeah," he said again.

A few weeks later, Milo left Reno once again. None of us heard from him until Dad received a postcard dated July 23, 2001. It was postmarked from a place in the Florida Keys called Marathon.

Dear Dad,
I'm finally getting used to this HUMIDITY – a Doctor told me once that he thought I had Rumatism [sic] *– I was sore all over, working in Reno, but here no pain at all! You can call me at Pizza Hut in Marathon—I don't have a Phone.*
Love, Milo

Enclosed was a copy of a letter to the OPINION section of the *Florida Keys Keynoter*. It was dated July 2, 2001, and any bad spelling had been corrected:

Despite stigma of presidential election, Florida's the place!

EDITOR:
This place is a tourist trap. I'm from the sin sick state of Nevada, with gambling, legal prostitution, and the highest rate of teen pregnancy in the nation.

> *I'm trapped here by loving, moral residents, who'll offer a stranger a beer, local officials who care about people and not special-interest agendas, and a high-tech Sheriff's Office that rivals the No. 1 police force, Miami-Dade. This is my third vacation here and I'm going to make Key West my family's permanent home.*
>
> *As great as Florida is, you still have the stigma of the presidential election. But don't be too hard on Secretary of State Harris. The problem started way back in her home town of Key West, as a first-grade straight-A student.*
>
> *One day she brought home an F. An enraged Mr. Harris demanded an explanation from the teacher. "Mr. Harris, Katherine is a well-behaved, intelligent, model student. She just can't count."*
>
> *John Reese*

Many months later, while on parole, Milo would write inflammatory letters to newly elected Congresswoman Katherine Harris. It was his luck that she did not press charges.

~~~

Excessive writing is yet another common behavior (of mania) ... Most of us who provide care for individuals with severe psychiatric disorders have received letters in which envelopes are covered with various messages, often written with different colored pens, at odd angles, and with messages on top of each other. Mania is the only psychiatric diagnosis that can be determined with 99 percent certainty without even opening one's correspondence.

– *Surviving Manic Depression*, by E. Fuller Torrey, M.D. and Michael B. Knable, D.O., Basic Books, 2002, p. 30

fa . nat . ic (f . nat . ik), noun. 1: a person with an extreme and uncritical enthusiasm or zeal, as in religion or politics ... Synonym 1: enthusiast, zealot, bigot, hothead, militant ... Fanatic and zealot both suggest excessive or overweening devotion to a cause or belief. Fanatic further implies unbalanced or obsessive behavior.
– *The Random House Dictionary of the English Language*, Second Edition Unabridged, Random House, Inc., 1987

Chapter Thirty-Two: Preparations in Florida

July 2001

It was a hot July morning in Marathon, Florida. At seven-thirty the men were already sweating as they learned against the garbage truck drinking their coffee. Fernando and Raphael were talking in Spanish, wondering why Nicolas had not yet arrived. Just as Fernando was about to walk over to the office to tell the boss, they spotted a tall, Anglo man coming toward them.

"Hi. I'm John Reese," he said, "and I'm going to work with you guys."

"*No comprendo, Señor.*" Raphael shrugged his shoulders.

"Well, I'll try my high school Spanish," Milo said, mostly to himself. *"Buenos días, me llamo Juan Miguel."*

* * *

During the morning, using Spanish, English, and mime, the three workers evolved themselves into a team. For the first part of the day, Fernando drove the truck. Raphael and Milo (Juan Miguel) hung onto the back, swinging off to run for barrels to empty into the huge truck bed. Raphael then switched on the mechanism which compressed the trash, and they were on to the next stop.

After two hours, the men would change places, Raphael driving, Fernando and Milo doing the running. Following lunch, it would be Milo's turn to drive.

Gradually, Milo learned that Fernando and Raphael were from Cuba. They implied that they had arrived here in some kind of small boat. During the noon break, they offered Milo some of their pork sandwiches, but he declined and pulled out cold pizza and a can of Coke from his large paper sack. He finally managed to explain that he had an evening job as a delivery driver for the local Pizza Hut.

Throughout the next few weeks, as Milo learned a bit more Spanish, he urged Fernando and Raphael to tell him about Cuba. They were eager to describe its geography and customs, its climate, its foods.

Cuba is just south of the Tropic of Cancer, 170 kilometers southwest of the tip of the Florida Keys. It is one of the largest islands in the world, with many natural bays and beaches. Forested mountains alternate between lush plains, where sugarcane shares space with grazing cattle. Cuba's temperature varies only ten degrees during the year – from the 70s to the high 80s, and its only seasons consist of a rainy summer and relatively dry winter.

Milo was surprised that most Cubans earned such a low monthly wage – the peso equivalent of ten dollars. But this was supplemented by a ration card, a *libreta*, to be used at government stores. This card entitled each Cuban to subsidized prices on certain amounts of selected basic items like rice, beans, and coffee.

Both Fernando and Raphael had harvested sugar cane in Cuba, but collecting garbage in Florida was an easier job, and it paid many times more. They talked about relatives back home, and they hoped someday to bring their families to the United States. Meanwhile, they sent home as much money as they could. But when Milo asked what they thought of Fidel Castro or the present-day Cuban government, the men were silent.

Milo wondered if they might be afraid that he would report them to American Immigration. He tried to put them at ease when he told them things were in the works that would make everything all right, and they would be welcome in both countries soon.

On August 28, 2001, Maria Siscar-Simpson heard pounding on the door of her condo in Delray Beach, Florida. She recognized the two young men outside as those she had recently seen around the complex. When they asked to come through her living room to retrieve a rolled-up bundle they had dropped from their balcony above, Ms. Siscar-Simpson refused. They were about to force their way in when the maintenance man yelled at the men and they reluctantly went away. Siscar-Simpson did not answer when she heard them return and knock again.

Two weeks later, on September 11, 2001, these same men would be forcing themselves into the cockpit of United Airlines Flight 93.

Besides Ahmad Al Haznawi and Ahmed Alnami, twelve other hijackers were in Florida during the months before 9-11. Some of them rented a 1996 white Ford Escort from Warrick's Rent-A-Car in Pompano Beach. A group of them stayed at the Panther Motel in Deerfield Beach.

Mohamed Atta and Marwan al-Shehhi took flying lessons at Huffman Aviation in Venice, Florida. After receiving commercial pilot's licenses, they moved to Opalocka, on the east coast of Florida, where they paid to practice on a Boeing 727 simulator.

Some of them purchased airline tickets shortly before September 11 on a computer at Kinko's in Hollywood, Florida.

The night of September 8, 2001, Atta, al-Shehhi, and another man spent an evening out at an oyster bar in Hollywood, Florida. Al-Shehhi reportedly drank five screwdrivers. When they checked out of their motel room in Deerfield Beach the next day, the men left behind their flight manuals and maps of the eastern United States.

~~~

[One] NIMH-funded study found a high co-occurrence of PTSD [post-traumatic stress disorder] and obsessive-compulsive disorder (OCD) among patients with bipolar disorder across a 12-month period. While the course of PTSD was independent of the mood disorder, the course of OCD frequently waxed and waned along with mood episodes.
 – *Bipolar Disorder Research at the National Institute of Mental Health, Fact Sheet,* 2004, http://www.nimh.nih.gov/publicat/bipolarresfact.cfm

Part Eight:

The Fall of Icarus – A Trip to Cuba

Oh that I had wings like a dove!
For then would I fly away, and be at rest.

– Psalms 55:6

The Dove

*Floating, swirling, sailing
down you came
Oh what a prize
never to tame.*

*Fit for her mission
like a satin glove
Sent from heaven
God's creature of love.*

*On life's gridded path
of unrest they don't know
The peace that I find,
I cry, 'stay, don't go!'*

*Feathered fame
sets her course
For clouds of victory
with my burden, remorse.*

*But n'er I'll forget
this little gift
From a higher will
my soul to lift.*

– John Reese
1982

Whenever the stories of families of the seriously mentally ill reach our national consciousness, it has been in the context of "newsworthy" tragedies. Reluctantly, we see ourselves and our loved ones in the newspaper headlines that both inform and mislead the general public.
— *I Am Not Sick I Don't Need Help*, Xavier Amador, Ph.D., Vida Press, 2000, p. 10

Chapter Thirty-Three: The Headlines

August 2001

Oscar usually went to the Senior Center in Minden for lunch. Once in awhile, he would go back to the Nugget buffet in Carson City, where he'd eaten his noon meal for years. But the Nugget had recently raised the price to $5.95, even with the discount for people over sixty-two. At the Senior Center, he could get a good meal for a couple of dollars and also meet people, sometimes interesting people.

Even at eighty-six, he was still handsome and never lacked attention from the ladies. Oscar had invited one woman for ice cream at the Country Store where he lived in Genoa. He had showed her around and pointed out the oldest bar in the state, the historic cemetery, the new golf courses, and his house on the mountain overlooking the town.

Today, Wednesday, Aug. 1, he arrived early for lunch and took a seat in the entryway to read the newspapers. He had cancelled *The New York Times* and *The San Francisco Chronicle* the day after Charlotte died. Now he had found the Senior Center, and there was usually at least one copy of the *Reno Gazette-Journal* sitting on the coffee table.

'Scared' U.S. Pilot Crash-Lands in Cuba

HAVANA (Reuters) – A U.S. pilot who said he was too scared to land in the Florida Keys on his first solo flight on Tuesday headed south for Cuba, where his plane overturned in a crash-landing on the coast.

Oscar stared at the front page. Even without his glasses, he recognized the photo of his son, Milo John Reese. There was another picture of a small plane, upside down on a beach somewhere, with people standing around it.

The Reuters article went on to say that the plane was a Cessna 172 and that it had crashed in rocky terrain near the sea. The lone pilot, who was shaken and bruised, was escorted away by police and was taken to a local hospital.

The article pointed out that there had been a history of illegal trips to and from Cuba. The Cuban government was hinting that this might be the latest in a series of political "stunts" by Cubans and Americans.

Paradise Aviation, a flight school in Marathon, Florida, identified the pilot as Milo John Reese, a man in his early fifties. A spokesperson for the flight school had no idea why the student pilot might have flown the $60,000 plane to Cuba. She said that this was his first solo flight and that it had involved circling the airport and landing the plane.

When Reese radioed the ground that he was afraid to land, she said, the instructor tried to talk him down.

"Then, about 100 yards out, he turned toward the ocean and didn't come back."

From then on, the pilot did not answer radio calls, but "he looked like he knew what he was doing."

Witnesses on the ground in Cuba, one hundred miles south of the Keys, said that a tire burst as the plane came in to land on the rocky beach, and then it turned over. "He (the pilot) looked all right, but a bit scared." said Johan Mora, a local resident.

"He was lucky, because he was going really close to the sea before he reached the ground," said Fabian Alejandro Molina Herrera, another witness to the crash.

A State Department spokesperson said that a Navy plane had tried to make contact with the pilot, to no avail. The U.S. Interests Section in Havana had been alerted. Meanwhile, the Cuban government was not giving out any details on the case. The spokesperson made the point that in the years since the Cuban revolution, with a few exceptions, most flights had been persons leaving Cuba, not the other way around.

In another article on the same day, the Associated Press stated that the pilot was not required to file a flight plan with air traffic controllers. Laura Brown, of the Federal Aviation Administration, said that all small aircraft would be operating under visual flight rules. Thus, there would be no record of the plane's intended route.

News media revealed that Milo John Reese was a delivery driver for Pizza Hut in Marathon. He had not reported to work Tuesday.

Oscar had not heard from Milo in weeks. That was not unusual. But there *had* been a phone message from Milo's wife this morning. She had just said to call her, but Oscar had chosen to put it off. He had figured that Milo probably needed money, either to pay the rent or to fix up the old car that he was now driving. The one they had recently bought was repossessed.

The last conversation with Milo had given a clue. At the time, Milo had told him that he liked Las Vegas a lot, and he was thinking about going there. Oscar suspected that Milo was getting sick; when Milo got sick, he took trips. Oscar had asked him if he was taking his pills.

"Sure," Milo had said, giving his now-standard answer. "But I really don't need 'em anymore."

Oscar read the article three times. Then he got up and started to leave. When he was just outside the door, Marge, the lady he had treated to ice cream, called his name.

He kept on walking, toward his old truck in the parking lot, and decided he could go without lunch today.

~~~

In its extreme forms mania is characterized by violent agitation, bizarre behavior, delusional thinking, and visual and auditory hallucinations.
   – Touched with Fire: Manic Depressive Illness and The Artistic Temperament, by Kay Redfield Jamison, Copyright 1993. Reprinted with the permission of The Free Press, a division of Simon & Schuster Adult Publishing Group

Sometimes, severe episodes of mania ... include symptoms of psychosis [or psychotic symptoms] ... Psychotic symptoms in bipolar disorder tend to reflect the extreme mood state at the time. For example, delusions of grandiosity, such as believing one is the President or has special powers...may occur.
   – National Institute of Mental Health, 2001, http://www.nimh.nih.gov/publicat/bipolar.cfm

Chapter Thirty-Four: The Pizza Pilot

I left Reno on July 1, 2001, with $50. I stopped in Las Vegas, Kingman, Arizona, Austin, Texas and Pensacola, Florida. I worked odd jobs in order to make enough money to reach my destination of Marathon, Florida. When I reached Marathon, I worked for a trash company in the morning and delivered pizza at night to make enough money to take flying lessons at $140 each. I slept in my car in a parking lot. An hour before my eighth lesson, I recall having a dab of Milwaukee's Finest.

Florida newspapers such as *The Miami Herald* reported that Milo's plane had crashed near Cojímar, a fishing village outside Havana where Ernest Hemingway had once kept his yacht. A State Department spokesperson stated that the U.S. government was currently in contact with Cuban authorities. The name Milo had first given the Cubans, Juan Miguel, was the same name as the father of Elian Gonzalez, the small lone survivor of a raft which had crossed from Cuba to the United States. There was a huge political upheaval when he was sent back.

The media learned about Milo John Reese's background. They found out that he was from Nevada, had been an anti-prostitution zealot, and had once staged his own disappearance.

At the time of the flight, Milo was working at Pizza Hut across from the Marathon Airport and staying in the Seaward Motel. Sheriff's deputies had found a book in his room there titled *How to Fly Cessnas*. There were interviews with people from the two flight schools at the Marathon Airport. The people at the first flight school Milo attended, Grant Air, had stopped giving him lessons because, they said, he was "flaky."

Rob Grant, the owner, stated, "As we say in the business, he was flying with a broken wing."

The F.B.I. had also interviewed Ed Steigerwald, the owner of Paradise Aviation, where Milo's flight had originated. He described Milo as a normal, capable student pilot that had logged twenty flight hours with this flight school. Steigerwald's wife said that during the flight, when Milo had told the ground that he could not land, the instructor had tried to talk him down. He simply replied, "Gosh, I'm scared."

The plane was on approach toward the runway when "the pilot suddenly pulled up, increased his speed and turned right, eventually heading southwest over the Keys—toward Cuba." From then on, there was no response on his radio.

Interviews with David Patten, Milo's only friend in Marathon, revealed that, on the day of the flight, the two had had lunch together, including two beers. Then he had invited Patten to accompany him on a flight to Key West.

"He didn't say Cuba," Patten said. "No mention of Cuba. I don't believe he even knew how far it was. Is it possible he did it to be famous?"

Major Douglas Martin, of the North American Aerospace Defense Command in Colorado Springs, said that they had tracked

Milo's plane. However, its direction, going away from the United States toward Cuba, was not as alarming as something coming in from Cuba would have been. In noting that there was no response from the Cubans, he also said, "They did not scramble MIGs [Russian fighter planes used by Cuba]."

The Miami Herald had interviewed experts who had said that Milo would likely have to remain in the hands of the Cuban government, although the plane itself might be returned to the United States. Wayne Smith, a retired U.S. diplomat who had worked in Cuba, said that in the past, offenders such as airline hijackers were sometimes "put out to cut sugar cane."

Back in Nevada, the *Reno Gazette-Journal* interviewed George Flint, the brothel lobbyist. He said that this latest act by John Reese did not surprise him. He had watched Milo's publicity stunts "grow increasingly erratic in the past 14 years ... I feel guilty even talking about the guy, he's such a loose cannon," Flint said. "He is getting exactly what he wants: attention."

Flint theorized that Milo might have flown to Cuba thinking that, from there, he could travel to Brazil to find Joe Conforte, the former owner of the Mustang Ranch who fled there to avoid charges of income tax evasion. Reese had called the *Reno Gazette-Journal* in the past, claiming that Conforte was being held in federal detention in Florida, but this proved not to be true. He had repeatedly contacted George Flint and made accusations against Conforte, asking where he could find him.

The news media went on to chronicle Milo's past high jinks in Nevada, such as chaining himself to the entrance of a health facility in Nevada and applying for a permit to open a gay brothel. It described how he had staged his own "abduction" a few years ago in order to call attention to his anti-brothel campaign.

One article had a unique take on the event. The August 1, 2001, issue of the *Bible Doctrine News* listed some of the facts and connected each one to biblical symbolism. "The name Milo may be derived from the Latin Miles, which means soldier, but it is also spelled basically the same as the Millo in the Bible. The Millo was the stronghold, or citadel, of the City of David, which is in Ophel in southeastern Jerusalem. Millo means fullness, or that which fills."

The author found almost every fact of the story heavy with symbolism. Florida was linked with the Palestinians; the model of the Cessna, 172, stood for law and order; and Cuba stood for "Simeon criminality."

Milo John Reese was from Nevada, the article said, which was the "region of the outcast, or garbage pit, which corresponds to the Dung Gate of Jerusalem."

Fly South Aviation News Africa reported that the Cuban Foreign Ministry stated that Cuban officials were conducting a "rigorous investigation" into the crash landing. Richard Boucher, of the U.S. State Department, said that this incident did not seem political. He said that, after suffering minor injuries from the crash, Milo John Reese was undergoing tests by Cuban doctors. The U.S. Interests Section in Havana was in touch with Reese's family.

There were speculations that Milo had had more flying experience than he had let on, and that he might have had a motive for taking the plane to Cuba. The *Associated Press* interviewed Ed Steigarwald, Milo's flight instructor from Paradise Aviation.

"We did not discuss any forms of navigation, especially long-range navigation," Steigarwald said. "He obviously had some prior experience, somewhere along the way."

At the State Department daily press briefing on August 2, Richard Boucher was asked about "the guy who flew to Cuba."

"The guy who flew to Cuba. Let's see," he replied. "As he will henceforth be known—yes, that's right. Soon to be a major motion picture [laughter in the audience].

"We are working with Cuban authorities on the next steps," responded Boucher to the next question, "including Mr. Reese's return to the United States and the disposition of the aircraft. In addition, Cuban authorities are investigating the crash."

In an article that same day, the Associated Press reported that the Cuban government employed a crane to move the Cessna 172 from where it had come down. They would then disassemble its parts in order to take them to a site for more investigation.

Interviews by *The Miami Herald,* with several doctors who sign medical forms for student pilots, revealed that some of these prospective pilots lie when it comes to drug use or alcohol abuse. And they often lie when it comes to the question that asks whether they suffer "mental disorders of any sort. Depression, anxiety, etc." If the person acts normal, there is no follow-up if the applicant answers in the negative.

"Essentially," said one doctor, "the F.A.A. relies on student pilots to be truthful in what amounts to an honor system."

There are twenty-two questions on the medical form. An F.A.A. spokesperson said that this agency did not know how Milo had answered those questions concerning his mental health. They were in the process of checking to see if the document had even been forwarded to their headquarters in Okalahoma City.

Milo had arrived at Paradise Aviation with the form, and the instructor had checked to see if a physician had signed it. Personnel at the flight school could not be sure whether the form had been signed by a physician from Florida or Nevada. The flight school no longer had the form.

Dr. William Schmidt, a physician in Miami, is with the F.A.A. and trained in checking the mental health of applicants. "You hope they are going to be truthful," he said. "But sometimes they are not."

Dr. Schmidt, a pilot himself, stated that false answers on the health questionnaire are punishable by up to five years in prison and a $25,000 fine. Nevertheless, he said, people lie on the forms.

Another physician, Dr. George Wright of Key Largo, also an F.A.A. examiner, said that when they find manic depression, they disqualify applicants because of their unpredictability. Although some mental illnesses are easy to detect, "with manic depression, when [patients] are under control, they can be very normal."

An aviation safety professor at Embry-Riddle University in Prescott, Arizona, said that, besides physicians, "The flight instructor [also] walks a tightrope in detecting mental illness."

Richard W. Bloom, a clinical psychologist at Embry-Riddle, said that mental health professionals should have a larger role in determining if an applicant is qualified to become a pilot.

"The trouble is, doctors don't always have psychology training," he said, adding, "Is it cost effective?"

Psychiatrists and psychologists rely on the...Diagnostic and Statistical Manual of Mental Disorders to make diagnoses (DSM-IV; American Psychiatric Association 1994a, 2000). Note the term "manual" in the title: A clinician should be able to pick up the manual and decide whether a patient meets the criteria for a specific psychiatric illness. Applying these diagnostic criteria reliably...cannot be done quickly or haphazardly: it requires considerable training, experience, and skill ...

– *The Bipolar Disorder Survival Guide*, by David J. Miklowitz, PhD, The Guilford Press, New York/London, 2002, p. 31

Feelings of religious inspiration are very common. Patients may feel that they are a modern prophet, the founder of a new religion, a reincarnation of Christ, even a new god.
  – *Bipolar Disorder: A Guide for Patients and Families*, Francis Mark Mondimore, M.D., Johns Hopkins University Press, 1999, p.12

Chapter Thirty-Five: Repercussions

I was pulled from the plane by a Cuban who told me to be quiet and not answer any questions. I was taken to a hospital and then to a luxury hotel in Havana. While there, I was questioned by Cuban officials. I knew I was in trouble, and I didn't want to come back to the U.S. They told me I could go anywhere; Mexico, etc. Then people from the U.S. Interests Section talked me into going home.

On August 3, 2001, in *The Miami Herald*, there was an article speculating that Milo John Reese might be returned to the United States soon. Authorities could charge him with violating Cuban airspace, and it was almost certain that he would have to face the charge of the theft of the plane.

The Herald said, "Forays to Cuba have been the source of heightened federal scrutiny since two exile planes were shot down by Cuban MIGs in 1996 ... The shoot-down prompted President Clinton to issue an order prohibiting entry into Cuban airspace or waters without U.S. permission. Violators could face up to 10 years in prison and fines of $10,000."

Jose Basulto, of Brothers to the Rescue, lost his pilot's license after the 1996 incident in which he was accused of flying into Cuban airspace. In an interview, he was angry that Americans are not allowed to go, even if they were born in Cuba. American Civil Liberties Union attorney Joseph Geller said that persons such as Milo should not be prosecuted for disobeying the presidential decree.

However, Miami prosecutors were more concerned with charging Milo with theft of the plane than where he flew it. Said one of them, Kendall Coffey, "He stole an aircraft; it doesn't matter whether he took it to Cuba or Cleveland."

Meanwhile, in Marathon, it was learned that around midnight on July 10, before Milo flew to Cuba, a local sheriff's deputy had found him sleeping in his car on the side of the Vaca Cut Bridge. He was told that he was trespassing and given a verbal warning.

In late July 2001, Milo had sent a letter to George Flint, his longtime adversary in Reno.

I'm tire [sic] *of getting laughed at by my friends, the press, and ostresized* [sic] *from avery* [sic] *church I try to attend ... It seems everyone in the state of Nevada hates me because I tried to close a whore house. It really does not make sence* [sic] *to me ... I'm never setting foot in Nevada again. This means a divorce from Susie because she refuses to move here.*

I have two jobs, one at Pizza hut and one with Marathon garbage services. I sometimes sleep in my car to save money.
   John Reese

The day after he mailed this letter, Milo flew to Cuba.

Frank Mullen, of the *Reno Gazette-Journal*, was interviewed by the *Citizen Free Press* on August 8. He portrayed

Milo John Reese as a "troubled man." He described him as "one of those zealots whose cause consumes them."

At some point, Milo called Mullen in Reno and mentioned that he was doing "important work" in Florida. "He saw himself as a private investigator-type," Mullen said. "He has always been... publicity hungry ... You can bet that whatever reason he has for going to Cuba will be completely off the wall."

August 6, 2001
Dear Dad (or so-called Expert Flight Instructor),

Well, Boss, this is a fine mess you got me into. I was at 300 degrees off the Cuban coast wondering where I would put this airplane down – during your professional flying instruction, you covered everything but landing on a reef of rocks. But, since you're my Dad, I'll let it slide.

I'm in a very plush hotel in the Historical District in downtown "Old Havana." I guess I'll be going back home soon.
 Love, Milo
 "Great Hotel"
 Havana, Cuba

In a letter to the editor of the *Marathon Free Press* that week, Brad Neat, another flight instructor at Paradise Aviation, also countered the rumors that Milo John Reese had not been competent to fly. He said that at Paradise Aviation, Milo had shown considerable flying skills, passed the written test, and indeed was ready to solo. Mr. Neat theorized that the landing in Cuba would have been successful had it not been for the large rock that overturned the plane. After all, Milo walked away from the site, and that was an accomplishment for any student pilot.

By August 8, newspapers were reporting that Milo John Reese would indeed be returned to the United States, and that he was scheduled to arrive at Miami International Airport that afternoon. Sheriffs deputies had a warrant out for his arrest for the theft of the $60,000 plane.

Bryan Hanson, of Paradise Aviation, was quoted as saying, "Hopefully, he's going to jail when he gets back."

The Miami Herald learned that the U.S. Interests Section had been working with the Cuban government while Milo was detained. The Cubans had now decided that the incident was probably not politically motivated, and they had decided to return him to the United States.

More interviews with Milo's wife, Susan, in Reno revealed that he had recently been prescribed a new drug, Valporic Acid. When the pills made him nauseated, his dosage was cut in half. Under the financial stress of needed car repairs, broken household appliances, and the $400 deposit they were required to pay their landlord for their new dog, Milo had cracked. He quit his job at a Reno kitty litter factory, got in his 1991 turquoise Suzuki, and drove to Las Vegas. He left his medication behind on the kitchen table.

In Las Vegas, Milo had taken flying lessons. He sent postcards to his wife Susan, and he called her every day.

"When he has a manic episode, he goes out flying," she said.

During this time, Susan had called the flight schools in Las Vegas. She told them about Milo's mental condition, and he was grounded there. After that, he headed for Florida.

The August 9 issue of the *Reno Gazette-Journal* reported that Milo John Reese was accompanied by three Cuban officials to an airport in Havana earlier that day. He looked cheerful and rested and carried a copy of *Granma*, the Cuban Communist newspaper. He then boarded a chartered jet and was flown to Miami.

When Milo stepped onto the runway at Miami International, he was immediately handcuffed, arrested by F.B.I officials, and escorted to a gray sedan. The charge: transportation of a stolen aircraft. The accompanying photo showed him wearing a plaid blue shirt and white pants, his eyes squinting under the glare of the sun, and his hands awkwardly bound in front of him. He was no longer smiling.

Agents drove Milo to the Federal Detention Center in Miami, where he was scheduled to have a hearing that afternoon before a U.S. Magistrate. Besides the federal charges, he would also face grand theft counts in Monroe County for stealing the plane.

One reporter for *The Miami Herald* wrote that after being arrested by F.B.I. agents, John Reese requested a meal. Referring to the fact that he had been wearing his Pizza Hut delivery uniform when he crashed in Cuba the week before, he asked for "No pizza, please." They gave him a Burger King Whopper.

The Cubans had released Milo because they could not find an ulterior motive for his entrance into Cuba, but Cuban Foreign Minister Felipe Perez Roque said that it was fortunate that no human life was lost in the incident. "We gave him the proper treatment, medical and otherwise, and all the facilities to return to the United States."

Indeed, Milo said, "They treated me like a king."

Fellow passengers on the chartered Gulf Stream International Airlines jet were troubled that Milo John Reese was allowed to fly without an escort. He had even made his way to the cabin during the flight to converse with the pilot.

Angel Infante, of Hialeah, Florida, later talked to reporters and expressed the anger he felt about the trip with Milo on board: "Let me tell you, I'm very upset this man was allowed to travel on a plane like that after what he did. It was very unnerving for those of us on the plane. What if he decided to do the same thing [again]?"

On the afternoon of August 9, 2001, Milo appeared in front of U.S. Magistrate Judge Robert L. Dube. Judge Dube asked, "Mr. Reese, do you have an attorney?"

Milo sat mutely in his seat.

"Mr. Reese, you have to answer. Do you have a lawyer to defend you?"

Milo turned his head to the wall. Still no answer.

Judge Dube then appointed a public defender and set arraignment for August 23. Milo would be held in the Miami Federal Detention Center until then without bond.

On his way out of the courtroom, Milo turned and winked at the spectators.

In Cuba, official Perez Roque promised that the Cessna would be returned to the United States "down to the last screw."

The Perspectives section of the August 13, 2001 issue of *Newsweek*, had this:

"Ed, this doesn't feel right." – Final radio transmission of novice pilot Milo John Reese, who took off for his first solo flight around a Florida airport but instead flew 100 miles before crash-landing in Cuba."

Rash acts during manic moods can have devastating consequences, such as financial ruin, divorce, and serious legal problems, any of which may be followed by severe guilt-ridden depression.

– *A Primer on Mental Disorders: a Guide for Educators, Families, and Students*, Thomas E. Allen, M.D., Mayer C. Liebman, M.D., Lee Crandall Park, M.D., and William C. Wimmer, M.D. Scarecrow Press, Inc. 4720 Boston Way, Lanham, Maryland 20706, 2001, p. 46, www.scarecrowpress.com

How many people with severe mental illnesses are in jails and prisons on any given day? If such illnesses are defined to include only schizophrenia, manic-depressive illness, and severe depression, then approximately 10 percent of all jail and prison inmates appear to meet these diagnostic criteria. The most recent data available in 1995 indicated there were 483,717 inmates in jails and 1,104,074 inmates in state and federal prisons in the United States, a total of 1,587,791 prisoners.

– *Out of the Shadows*, E. Fuller Torrey, M.D., John Wiley and Sons, Inc., 1997, p.31

Chapter Thirty-Six: Aftermath

Milo appeared in court on Tuesday, August 14, 2001, in front of Judge Barry Garber. The prosecuting attorney, Kim Selmore, gave some background facts concerning the defendant. He had disappeared from his home in Reno, Nevada, on June 14, 2001. His wife, Susan, had not known his whereabouts until the day of his flight to Cuba when she received a call from the F.B.I.

Arguing for detention, Selmore stressed the nature of the crime. She pointed out that when Navy pilots tried to locate him, the defendant "made a number of evasive moves which placed those pilots in danger."

By crashing the plane near a road in Cuba, Ms. Selmore claimed that he had endangered the lives of people there. Milo had offered to take a friend on this flight with him, and he might have endangered that person's life as well.

The witness for the government was Anthony Russo of the Federal Bureau of Investigation. Celeste Higgins, the defendant's attorney, asked Russo if he was aware of any previous flying experience on the part of the defendant. Russo answered that there were some indications Milo had flown in the area of his home, in Reno, Nevada. He had also taken lessons during a trip to Florida three years before, at Marathon Airport, with Grant Air. But none of these lessons included solo flights.

Mr. Russo described the route which the plane took. "He flew along the coast of the Keys at a heading of about 240 degrees … for the Yucatan Peninsula until he got to Key West. Maybe about 25 to 50 miles off Key West, the Navy P3 made visual contact with Mr. Reese. Somewhere in that time frame he changed his heading from the 240 heading out toward the Yucatan Peninsula to 180, which is directly south toward Havana."

Agent Russo also testified that Milo had shouted over the radio that his hands were cold or frozen. "He landed at the first land," he said. "And that was Cuba."

Ms. Selmore asked Russo for details regarding Reese's offer to take a friend with him on the day of the flight. Russo named the friend as David Patton, who had declined Reese's offer because he had to go to work that day. Agent Russo thought that would have needed to be cleared by Paradise Aviation, anyway.

On the redirect examination, Mr. Russo said he had interviewed Rob Grant, the owner of Grant Air, where Milo had taken previous flight training. Grant described his flying as "very smooth, air show smooth."

Celeste Higgins, the public defender, argued that Milo had performed all the things he was supposed to do until he panicked and went out over the water. There was, she said, no evidence of any alternative motive; he landed in Cuba because it was the next place he had crossed land. She insisted this was not a situation where one could simply turn around and come back.

There was no other motive but that the defendant wanted to land the airplane and did not know how to do it. He had not tried to hide his landing spot nor had he transported any items. He did not transport any individual. Milo John Reese, Ms. Higgins said, had no ties to Cuba, only to the United States. He had a family in Reno and enough ties in the U.S. to be released on bond.

The judge then asked the prosecuting attorney if the government was planning to ask for a psychiatric or psychological evaluation, and Ms. Selmore said yes. His reason for asking was that the defendant demonstrated erratic behavior prior to this incident, by "absconding and not...advising his family." The Court would wait to take any further action until it had the results of that evaluation.

Milo's medical records had not yet been sent from Nevada. Neither she nor the judge had an idea of the scope of Milo's illness.

Ms. Higgins advised the court that "Mr. Reese adamantly objects to any kind of implication that he has mental health issues."

Judge Garber responded that he was not implying that the defendant had mental health issues, and that if there was nothing found, then it would be to everyone's benefit to have it on the record. He then ordered Ms. Higgins to prepare an order for this evaluation, and she agreed to so. The subsequent order set the psychological evaluation for Tuesday, September 11, 2001.

On September 13, Milo had not yet been examined by a psychiatrist. The judge issued another order. This one spelled out, in more detail, that the defendant, Milo John Reese, "shall be examined by at least one qualified psychiatrist or psychologist... to determine if (he) is mentally competent to understand criminal proceedings against him and to properly assist in his defense."

During this time, the defendant would be in the custody of the Attorney General and remain in the Bureau of Prisons Detention Center in Miami, Florida. The judge also ordered a physical and neurological examination and stipulated that all these procedures must be conducted within the next thirty days.

September 20, 2001
Dad –

Thanks for the money and the letter – I put it in my commissary account. I called my attorney [Celeste Higgins] *and told her to get my Nevada* [medical] *records. They aren't giving me medication yet – I am being evaluated by the psychology dept.*

I told Susie to send my Volproic Acid to Marathon because I ran out – it never arrived. This prison isn't bad. There's a lot to do here.

Love, Milo

When Milo was finally given the tests, he submitted to the physical, which he passed. During interviews with the court-appointed psychiatrist, he would not say one word.

November 28, 2001
Dear Cyndi & Ted,
Thank you for your letters. I don't mind prison life. This place reminds me of a hotel. If we really clean up our unit we get extra privileges. One time we cleaned spotlessly and the warden almost gave her approval, but someone whistled at her. Oh, well. (She is very attractive.)
Love, Milo

October 15, 2001
Dear Dad,
Thanks for the money. I'm sending (Kevin) *the title to my car. I asked him to move to Marathon. His son, too.*

I think the judge is going to dismiss my case. If I get out you can write to me at my Marathon P.O. Box #.

They are probably going to make a movie about my experience.

I'll get some money, but I still want to go back to Marathon. The manager is real nice and I'm sure she'll give me my job back. I really want to live in Key West – its bigger than Marathon and there's a lot more to do, a lot of history there – Ernest Hemingway lore, etc.

Love, Milo

On January 31, 2002, Milo changed his mind again. He went before the Court to change his plea from "not guilty" to "guilty." He was sentenced to six months but given credit for time served. The Court also ordered restitution in the amount of $45,000. The defendant would be on "supervised release" for the term of three years. Milo was then put in the custody of the U.S. Marshall.

The judgment in the case of the United States v. Milo John Reese in the Southern Federal District of Florida spelled out the terms of the supervised release: The defendant must not leave his assigned judicial district without the permission of the court or probation officer; he must report to a probation officer each month and submit a written, truthful report; he must answer truthfully all questions by the probation officer, and he must support all dependents and meet family responsibilities, work regularly at a lawful occupation, and notify the probation officer at least ten days prior to any change of residence or employment. In addition, "the defendant shall not possess a firearm, destructive device, or any other dangerous weapon."

A payment of $100 toward the fine was due immediately. The U.S. Probation Office was ordered to set up a payment schedule for the rest of the $45,000 – ten percent from each paycheck when the defendant was again employed.

A few days after this court hearing, Milo John Reese boarded a Greyhound bus for Reno. No one had told him he could never again fly a plane.

~~~

While the causes for arrest of seriously mentally ill persons may vary, an underlying theme is the profound failure of the public mental health system to care for the seriously mentally ill. Despite millions invested by the federal government, the mental health system has not responded to the needs of those most acutely in need of services. As a result, thousands

find themselves in a different system – the criminal justice system.
– *Criminalizing the Seriously Mentally Ill, The Abuse of Jails as Mental Hospitals*, E. Fuller Torrey, Joan Stieber, Jonathan Ezekiel, Sidney M. Wolfe, Joshua Sharfstein, John H. Noble and Laurie M. Flynn; a joint report of the National Alliance for the Mentally Ill and Public Citizen's Health Research Group, 1992, p. 43-44

Part Nine:

Trail of Madness

We all are born mad. Some remain so.

– Samuel Beckett, *Waiting for Godot, Act I*

Mania is what makes bipolar disorder different ... And what makes mania is its energy. Sometimes it's a euphoric energy that propels you through life at breakneck speed ... And sleep? How can you possibly sleep when there's so much to do, so many profound insights to explore?... You feel as if you can accomplish just about anything. In fact, you know you will.
– *Taming Bipolar Disorder*, by Lori Oliwenstein, *Psychology Today Here to Help Series*, published by the Penguin Group, 2004, p. 6

Chapter Thirty-Seven: Coming to Terms

February 15, 2002

"Hello?"
"Hi, Milo. It's Cynthia."
"Hi, how're ya doing?"
"Fine. And thanks for the writing you sent. I can use it in the book."
"Say, about the book ..."
"Yes?"
"I don't think it should have a lot of psychological stuff. I think it should be mostly about my adventures."

"No way, Milo. Your illness can't be separated from your so-called adventures!"

"You know," Milo said, "there are a lot of people who wish they could do things like I've done, but they think they have too many responsibilities."

"Well, they *do* have responsibilities," I agreed. "But I guess I know what you mean, though. Sometimes I'm driving along on the freeway, on my way to work, and I look at the green hills, with the poppies in bloom, and I just wish I could keep going, though I don't."

"Yeah, you see, I have an excuse. You don't."

"What ... did ... you ... say?"

"I'm mentally ill, you're not."

"I see ..."

"A person can also do other things when they're manic, like concentrate on flying a plane."

"I guess you did *that*, didn't you?"

"And you really don't need much sleep when you're manic."

"Oh, yes," I remembered. "You told me that you walked from the Keys to Miami in one shot."

"Yeah. Marathon, Key Largo, Homestead ..."

"But didn't you even rest?"

"I sacked out a couple of hours in Homestead. I remember the cops shaking me awake."

"How long did it take you to get to Miami?"

"Let's see, I left Marathon about two one afternoon, and I got to the Port of Miami just before midnight the next day."

"My God. Did you walk all that way on that Highway One?"

"Mostly. I remember feeling a blow to my hand. I'd been hit by the rearview mirror on some car."

"You were lucky your hand was all that was hit. That was dangerous."

"Naw ... I've done things a lot more dangerous. That's another thing. When you're manic, you're not afraid of anything."

"Like crash-landing a plane on a rocky beach in Cuba."

"I've gotta' go to work now."

"Oh, yes. You got your old job back at Domino's in Reno."

"Yeah. I made eighty-five dollars in tips last night."

"Good. Are you going to put that money toward paying off your fine?"

"I'll talk to you later …"

"Okay. Goodbye, Milo."

During the spring of 2003, my sister Carolyn and I decided to visit Miami and the Florida Keys in order to find out more about our brother's infamous flight. We planned the trip for June, when each of us would be finished teaching for the year. Neither Carolyn nor I had ever been to Florida. Little did we know just how interesting it would be.

June 15, 2003

The phone was ringing.

"Hello?"

"Cynthia? Did I wake you up?"

"No, Dad. I have an early flight. I have to be at the airport at five."

"Well, I just thought I'd let you know. Milo left Reno yesterday for Florida."

"You're kidding." I gulped coffee. "He broke his probation? He just…*left*?"

"Yeah. Susan called last night."

"Milo's wife? Did she say whether he took his car, or did he fly?"

"She didn't say." I could hear the gloom in Dad's voice.

"Well, maybe we'll run into him in Miami."

"You could," he chuckled a bit.

"I'll call you when I get there, Dad."

Hours later, waiting for Carolyn at Miami International, I called Dad on my cell phone. He told me that he had gone to the Reno airport and found Milo's car in the parking lot.

"So now we know he took a plane," I said. "Dad, you missed your calling. You should have been a private investigator."

"Is Carolyn there yet?"

"As a matter of fact, here she comes. We'll call you when we get to the hotel, OK?"

I knew Carolyn hated flying, but her white face gave portent to the story she told. "Horrible flight. Not just bumpy. As we were approaching to land, all of a sudden the pilot pulled up. Scared the hell out of everybody. He came on the intercom in a routine, matter-of-fact tone of voice to say that we had to take evasive action concerning another plane."

"God, you need a drink, Sis!" I hugged her. "Remember, dinner's on me tonight. We're going to celebrate your tenure."

"And getting here in one piece," Carolyn muttered.

After checking into our rooms at the Holiday Marina Hotel, we ventured across a wide street to the Bayside Marketplace. Milo had told us about it after one of his other visits to Miami. Shops and restaurants circled the small harbor. In a central area it boasted live entertainment with Latin ambiance. On the far side, we could see the bridge to the Port of Miami and South Miami Beach.

We had gasped at the stifling heat and closeness of the air as we came out of the hotel; now we welcomed the slight breeze off the water at Snapper's bar. Carolyn had a glass of Chardonnay; I sipped a weak martini on the rocks.

"I'm so freaking mad at Milo," I said.

"Really?" Carolyn looked sideways at me. "I have lots of feelings about him, but anger isn't one of them. If anything, I feel afraid for him. Especially when he's out there on the streets."

"I'm furious at what he's put this family through. Especially what he's put Dad through. And I know it was terrible for Mom, all those years before she died. With these latest stunts, he's really gone over the top. It isn't just *us* he's affecting now."

Back at the hotel, I opened the drapes in my ninth-floor room. I could see twinkling lights from cruise ships, small cities in themselves.

It was time to call Dad.

~~~

At times, families can be particularly resentful if they perceive an episode as having been triggered by sufferer's stopping his or her mood stabilizers. This is a tricky issue as families can see their sick relative as being irresponsible.
   – *Coping with Bipolar Disorder: A Guide to Living with Manic Depression*, by Steven Jones, Peter Hayward and Dominic Lam, Oneworld Publications, England, 2002, pp. 101-102

The main reason that stopping...medication is inadvisable is that it is associated with a high risk of recurrence ... In fact, not taking medications, as prescribed, is the greatest single factor contributing to when and how often bipolar people have recurrences.
– *The Bipolar Disorder Survival Guide*, David J. Miklowitz, PhD. The Guilford Press, 2002, p. 132

Chapter Thirty-Eight: Miami Justice

June 16, 2003

The office of the Federal Public Defender of the Southern District of Florida occupies the entire seventeenth floor of 150 W. Flagler St. in Miami. Carolyn and I stepped off the elevator into a waiting room of black Italian leather couches arranged on an off-white carpet. The receptionist asked us who we were here to see.

"We have an appointment with Celeste Higgins," I said. "But we're a bit early. We can leave and come back."

"I'll tell her you're here."

A few minutes later, the door was opened by a tall woman who looked to be in her mid-thirties. Her hair was highlighted blonde, and she wore a summer knit suit that showed off her slim figure. She had the darkest brown eyes I had ever seen.

"Hello. I'm Celeste Higgins. You must be Cynthia."

"Yes, and this is my sister Carolyn."

"I have news," she said, as she ushered us into her corner office. Two banks of windows held a view of the west side of the city and the gathering clouds coming in from the Gulf.

"Milo showed up here at eight-thirty this morning and demanded to speak to me," she said.

"We knew he'd come to Florida, Ms. Higgins," I admitted. "We've been talking to our father."

"Call me Celeste. The receptionist reached me at home. I told her not to let him leave. He said that he wanted to turn himself in. But I guess he talked to someone else here in the meantime. They told him that, unless we have a warrant, we can't take him. He wouldn't be an official escapee without that warrant. So he left the office, and he's wandering downtown Miami."

"When we called Dad this morning," I said, "he said that he had talked to him late last night. Milo was hungry and out of money. Dad asked us to find him and put him on a plane back to Reno."

"Unfortunately," said Celeste, "the person here in the office told Milo that he would have to commit a serious offense in order to be taken into custody. I'm worried that he might do something drastic. Is he unbalanced again? Off his medication?"

"We never know for sure with Milo," I replied. "Our father went to see him at his landscaping job in Reno last week. Dad thought he was doing well. But Milo called me in Santa Barbara last Wednesday, and *I* thought he was higher than a kite. He started reading me this stuff he'd written, and it didn't make any sense."

"High? Does he take other drugs?"

"I mean 'high' like in mania," I said. "He has always had an aversion to any kind of drugs, including those he *should* be taking. He says it has to do with his having been an athlete in school."

"About the reason for your visit …" Then Celeste held up her hand to answer the ringing phone.

"Hi. Anything yet?" She covered the receiver with her hand and turned to us. "The Probation Department called the Marshall's Office. He hasn't shown up there." Celeste had a few more words of conversation and replaced the receiver.

There was a knock. The door opened, framing two muscular young men. The dark-haired one spoke.

"One of us is going next door. Can we bring you ladies anything? Cuban pastries?"

The three of us nodded in unison. When the men were gone, we resumed our interview.

"Last week, your brother sent me this book." Ms. Higgins held up a best selling paperback, *The Alchemist,* by Paulo Coehlo. "Then he called me to find out if I'd received it. He told me that he was madly in love with me. He said I was his soul mate. That I should leave my husband and marry *him*. So, when I heard he'd been here this morning, I called those investigators."

"Wow." I was finding out about a brother I did not know.

"But Milo's a gentle soul," Carolyn said. "No matter how sick, he has never been violent. I don't think ..."

"I've seen him angry," Celeste responded. "I don't want to be alone in my office if he comes back."

"When Milo called me, he was on his new cell phone." I handed her a crumpled piece of paper. "I wrote down the number. Here it is."

Celeste copied the number on a Post-it note.

"By the way," I remembered, "he also got a cell phone for our Dad. And I think that was another clue that he was manic – it was an extravagance he couldn't afford."

Celeste picked up the phone again and dialed Milo's number. "Mr. Reese," she said after a moment, "this is Celeste Higgins. It is very important that I speak with you. Please call me at my office."

"The cell phone probably ran out of juice," I offered. "Or he left it on the plane."

"Or he gave it away, along with any money left in his pockets," Carolyn agreed. "That's what he does when he gets sick. Gives everything away, sometimes even his car."

"After it runs out of gas," I said.

"What kinds of things would you like to know about what happened?" Celeste pointed to a manila folder. "Here are some newspaper accounts that I kept. I can make you copies."

"Thanks. We'd appreciate an overview of the case as you remember it."

"At first, this appeared to be an understandable situation of a student pilot afraid to land on his solo flight and just flying off. And that's what I told the newspapers, originally. It would have gone fine, if it weren't for the letter."

"The *letter*?"

"The one he left in his car the day of his flight. It stated his intention of flying to Cuba. That letter proved premeditation, and the prosecution picked up on it immediately."

"Of course."

"And then, of course, he wrote another letter from the Federal Detention Center while he was being held there. This one was to the Miami Herald telling about his intentions to kidnap and assassinate Castro. He signed the letter, 'The Pizza Pilot.'"

"*Assassinate*? This is the first we've heard of that, I said.

"We heard only the word 'kidnap!'" Carolyn interjected. "So much for our illusion of Milo as a gentle soul."

"If there had been a trial, I could have entered an insanity plea. No one in his right mind, without ties to Cuba, would plan an escapade like this. It would be senseless. But he refused to plead insanity. In fact, he was so against it he wrote me a letter stating that he wanted me 'out of his life.' He told me not to represent him any more. I recognized the manic pattern."

One of the bodyguards arrived with a large bag. Celeste thanked him, took out pastries and three covered Styrofoam cups. The coffee was steaming and laced with cream and sugar. The delectable smell reached our noses.

"Milo later changed his mind again and kept me on the case, but he insisted on a guilty plea rather than insanity. He said, 'I don't want to use my mental health as an excuse.' Period.

"I asked him," Celeste continued, "if he knew the ramifications of pleading guilty. He said yes. I told him that, as a convicted felon, he would lose his civil rights. He could not appeal his case, he could never vote again, never own a firearm."

I wouldn't mind Milo not having a firearm, I thought to myself, remembering that he had once held a gun to his head.

"Still, he insisted on pleading guilty."

"Tell us about the second letter. Where is it now?"

"*The Herald* has it. It was originally intercepted by the authorities, but someone on the inside probably leaked a copy. Then 9-11 happened, and no one seemed to care about the Pizza Pilot anymore. Except for the fact that he had taken a plane so easily."

"What happens now?" I asked.

"Well, he's violated his release. But he starts out at level one because he has no prior felony convictions. He'll serve some time, I would guess, three to nine months."

"Where?"

"Probably in Nevada. That's where the jurisdiction was."

"In a place where he can receive help?"

"Unfortunately, the criminal justice system is not equipped to look beyond the strict requirements of the law. The people in charge see their primary duty as punishing the offenders and protecting the rest of the public. They aren't well-equipped to deal with mental health issues. There is no question that your brother needs special help, but there are also the federal requirements of probation."

"When he's through serving these three to nine months, will he be put back on probation?"

Celeste nodded. "It's called 'supervised release.' That's the term given for someone who has been convicted and has served time. Probation is given to those who have never been incarcerated."

"Will he be back in a halfway house?"

"Probably. You know, he tried to get transferred to a halfway house here in Florida. I don't know why. These places are horrible …"

"Our Dad visited him in the one in Reno and said that it seemed to be decent. It looked clean and Milo liked the food. And they were *supposedly* making sure he took his medication. Guess he fooled them with his little 'put it in the back of his mouth to spit out later' trick."

"Sounds familiar. These bipolar people I see are all incredibly bright, capable, creative people. When they don't take their medication, they do stupid things. And law enforcement does not recognize 'stupid' as an excuse."

"Did you talk to the guy who taught him to fly?"

"I talked to man from the first flight school he went to in Marathon. After a few lessons, Milo told them that he'd had experience, and he wanted to solo. They said he was definitely not ready, that he had fudged on his flight log, and his forms were not complete. And they said that he acted 'flaky.' That's when he went across the airport to Paradise Aviation. When he presented himself there, he had fixed up his forms and didn't act flaky. That's why they gave him lessons."

As we went back through the sequence of events of that summer day almost two years ago, Celeste asked us to tell her more about Milo's illness.

"Growing up in the San Fernando Valley," I responded, "he was the perfect, All American Kid. Then, when he was a freshman in high school, our parents bought a ranch in Nevada."

"I've sometimes wondered if moving to the ranch had something to do with it," Carolyn said.

"He was diagnosed as schizophrenic when he first got sick," I continued. "That was during his freshman year at the University of Nevada. There wasn't much known about manic depression then, and the drugs they gave him were too strong – in fact, they almost killed him. Milo's had periodic bouts ever since. Even though the drugs have improved, they haven't helped him much."

"Of course," Carolyn said, "they won't help because he doesn't take them."

"When he called last week, he asked me personal questions," Celeste said. "Like, was I Cuban? I told him that my father was, but he died when I was two. Milo responded that he had lost his mother recently, and he knew how horrible it was to lose a parent. I told him that I was okay with my loss, that I didn't even remember my father. But he went on and on. He talked about how close he was to your mother. About how she was the only one who could persuade him to take his medication. After she died, he said, he 'let things go.'"

"Losing our mother was horrendous," Carolyn said. "She was wonderful, and we all felt the loss, but I hadn't realized that it was *that* extreme for Milo."

"Neither had I," I echoed. "However, now that I look back on things, it was after Mom died that his antics grew to be more and more 'out there.' He staged his own disappearance a couple of years after that. His manic episodes began to come more often, and they increased in intensity. And then, the trip to Cuba. While our mother was alive, Milo never broke the law – except for the time he chained himself to a public building in passive protest."

"He told me," said Celeste, "that his counselor had suggested that he apologize to the people he hurt, so maybe he was calling to make up for firing me that time. He called me several more times last week, but I wouldn't talk to him. Now I'm wondering if he came to Miami just to see *me*."

Carolyn and I stared at each other. We could not think of anything to say.

~~~

The unwillingness to see mental illness as a legitimate disease is evident in our legal system. In one highly visible trial after another, defendants, no matter how obviously disconnected from conventional reality, are judged responsible for their crimes and sent to prisons instead of hospitals. Only on rare occasions does the insanity defense succeed in court. We may acknowledge that mental illness is real, but we have trouble identifying and even more trouble excusing behavior because of it.

– *The Burden of Sympathy: How Families Cope with Mental Illness*, by David A. Karp, Oxford University Press, 2001, pp. 255-256

Many have the charm of youth and the stirring quality of a drink of champagne. Pueri aeterni are generally very agreeable to talk to ... They do not like conventional situations; they ask deep questions and go straight for the truth. Usually they are searching for genuine religion, a search that is typical for people in their late teens.
– *The Problem of the Puer Aeternus*, Marie-Louise Von Franz, edited by Daryl Sharp, Inner City Books, 2000, p. 9

Chapter Thirty-Nine: A Personal Legend

After we left the Public Defender's office, we walked to the District Court to make copies of documents about Milo's trial. On the way out, we saw the large, imposing gray building that was the Federal Detention Center for the Southern District of Florida. The windows on its fifteen stories were several feet high but only four to six inches wide. There was no mistaking this building from the others around it.

As we walked the streets, we ducked into air-conditioned shops for relief from the choking heat. We checked with three Western Union shops, where we left money and notes for Milo. At one point, Carolyn walked up to a security officer and asked him where skid row was. At his incredulous expression, we explained that we were looking for a particular person who was out of money but knew how to survive on the street.

"I don't think you two ladies should be going into the rough places in town. But you might try calling the homeless shelters."

We entered the library, cell phones in hand, to find a Miami phone book. After several calls, and no luck, we gave up and decided we'd done enough for one day.

One the way back to the hotel, I bought a copy of *The Alchemist*. That night, when I still couldn't sleep after watching three reruns of *Law and Order*, I picked up the book. As I read, I tried to understand Milo's fascination with this particular novel. After a few pages, I began to comprehend.

The Alchemist is the story of Santiago, an Andalusian shepherd boy. He leaves home to go in search of his dreams and his "personal legend." His journey takes him to Africa and, eventually, to the pyramids of Egypt. Along the way, during his many adventures, he learns to trust his heart and to read the signs which propel him toward his goal. He is taught to trust his intuition and look into his heart for answers to the secret of life. That secret has to do with living in the immediate moment.

A camel driver tells him, "I don't live in either my past or my future. If you can concentrate always on the present, you'll be a happy man."

Santiago crosses the desert in search of a treasure. Along the way, he meets a girl named Fatima, with whom he falls in love.

The book goes on: "When two...people encounter each other and their eyes meet, the past and the future become unimportant. There is only that moment."

Santiago learns to live each moment intensely. There is no regret in having given up his secure life as a shepherd. He eventually finds an alchemist, a man who can turn metal into gold.

When Santiago leaves Fatima, again to pursue his dreams, the alchemist tells him not to think about what he has left behind. "You must understand that love never keeps a man from pursuing his personal legend ... No heart has ever suffered when it goes in search of its dreams, because every second of the search is a second's encounter with God and with eternity."

The boy looks into his own soul, sees God, and realizes that he, a mere shepherd, can "perform miracles." He can even turn himself into the wind.

~~~

The increased…sense of importance that accompanies mania is another aspect [of bipolar disorder] … Increased sexual activity is also common … Sexual thoughts and feelings often become intermingled with the person's euphoria and delusional thinking.
– *Surviving Manic Depression*, E. Fuller Torrey, M.D. and Michael B. Knable, D.O., 2002, Basic Books, pp. 27-28

The truth is that impulsive and grandiose behavior rarely allows you to consider what you're doing in mid-mania ... much less question its legality. Add inhibition-stripping drugs and alcohol into the mix, or throw in delusions and hallucinations, and you've got a true emotional and behavioral powder keg.

– *Taming Bipolar Disorder*, A Psychology Today *Here to Help* book, by Lori Oliwenstein, Alpha Books, published by the Penguin Group, 2004, p. 224

Chapter Forty: Scene of the Crime

June 17, 2003

The weather report warned of strong thunderstorms expected in South Florida later that day. With this in mind, we rented an S.U.V. I drove; Carolyn navigated from the Triple A map. She pointed out the sign for Homestead.

"That's the town that was flattened by a huge hurricane," I said. "Milo went through Homestead when he walked the ninety miles from Marathon to Miami."

"How can anyone walk ninety miles?" Carolyn sighed.

The clouds turned darker, the color of iron. Just as the road narrowed to two lanes, sheets of rain blurred my vision. I turned the wipers on high, but the road ahead remained only a dim image.

Fortunately, in Florida they say, "If you don't like the weather, wait five minutes." By the time we had crossed the bridge into Key Largo, the sun was shining. We found a Subway in Islamorada and had a late lunch of reassuring, familiar food.

The Keys have one narrow, main thoroughfare, U.S. Highway 1. A dense growth of trees on either side is broken by short roads leading to small marinas. On the bridges, looking at the water, we understood why the Spanish had named this area Islamorada, or purple island. The surrounding water indeed had mauve tints, along with all varieties of aqua and ultramarine.

"You gotta hand it to Milo," Carolyn observed. "When he gets sick and travels, at least he picks beautiful places."

There were few cars today. "I'm glad we planned our visit in the middle of the week," I said.

But signs saying "Hurricane Shelter" reminded us of the all-too-real danger of living here. The traffic would be terrible in a mass evacuation.

We came to Marathon around three o'clock. The Holiday Inn sat at the edge of town, to our left. Agreeing to come back later to check in, we soon came to the Marathon Airport. It was small but adequate for the private Lear and Gulf Stream jet planes sitting beside its runway.

"We have an appointment there tomorrow to talk to Ed Steigerwald's crew chief, Steve Holmstrom," I said. "Steigerwald's the guy that used to own Paradise Air. He sold the business after Milo stole his plane. He doesn't want to see any of Milo's relatives, but he doesn't mind if Steve talks to us."

We kept driving. I spied the Pizza Hut, put on the brakes, and turned into the parking lot. "Let's see if anyone here remembers Milo," I said.

We found a young, plump girl inside. We asked her if she had worked with Milo. "Oh, the guy who flew to Cuba. No, I wasn't here then, but I'll get the manager. I think she remembers him."

A few moments later, a small dark woman came out from the back. Her nameplate said *Napharine*. We introduced ourselves and commented on her beautiful name. Would she be willing to speak to us about our brother?

"Well, all I can say is that he was a very dependable worker. Always showed up. Always on time. Until, of course, that day …"

"Anything else you can remember about Milo?"

"He had a friend who worked here, too. His name was David. Or Davy. Davy Patten."

I now remembered where I had heard that name. *The Miami Herald* had interviewed a David Patten about his lunch with Milo on the day of the flight. He said that Milo had ordered French fries and two Budweisers. The two beers Celeste had mentioned. Then Milo had asked Patten if he wanted to fly with him to Key West.

"I think Davy lives in the City Marina. It's a left turn across from the Overseas Liquor Store about a mile down the road."

We thanked Napharine and started driving south. Before we realized it, we were on the Seven Mile Bridge. So, with no place to turn around, we relaxed and enjoyed the experience – especially the travel-magazine view.

The clouds were almost gone by now. When we saw a small state beach at the other end of the bridge, we parked, took off our shoes, walked across the white sand, and waded into the Atlantic. There were other people in the water, too, some out hundreds of yards. I took a picture of Carolyn making a call to Ted on her cell phone. The warm, tropical waters swirled around her calves.

Back in Marathon, we made several passes before we found the City Marina. No one in the boathouse knew anyone named Davy Patten. We asked around awhile and finally gave up. The heat had won this round.

"Too bad we couldn't find that guy. He probably knew Milo better than anyone here."

It was almost seven when we unlocked our adjacent rooms at the Holiday Inn. Shortly after I had slipped on my bathing suit, I heard a knock at the door.

"I've discovered the best thing about this hotel, better than the swimming pool," Carolyn said. "Wait till you see the Tiki Bar!"

With its easterly breeze, the Tiki Bar was the coolest place we had been anywhere outdoors in Florida. It was a large grass hut with a giant bar overlooking yet another marina. Across the water were luxury homes and private docks.

"I swear, I've never seen so many boats. There must be more boats in the Florida Keys than there are people. Sailboats, rowboats, powerboats …"

"And don't forget charter boats, fishing boats, jet skis."

After a couple of Bud Lights on tap, we decided to skip a dip in the pool and have dinner.

"We could order a pizza," I teased. "Maybe Milo came down here and got his old job back again at Pizza Hut!"

~~~

Alcohol acts on the brain like a minor tranquilizer, relieving anxiety, restlessness, and hyperactivity. Most everyone knows how alcohol slows you down. For the manic or psychotic, this effect may be even more dramatic, and more welcoming.

– *We Heard the Angels of Madness: A Family Guide to Coping with Manic Depression,* by Diane and Lisa Berger, Quill Press / William Morrow, 1991, p. 115

It is not uncommon in the bursting of florid mania that a series of chance events…conspire with the nascent distortions of manic thinking to trigger behavior that catapults the illness into the public arena. Then, with events out of control, anything can happen. Frequently as the behavior escalates the police are called …and tragedy may not be far away.
 – *A Mood Apart: The Thinker's Guide to Emotion and Its Disorders*, by Peter Whybrow, M.D., Harper Perennial, 1998, p. 54

Chapter Forty-One: Profile of a Felony

Wednesday, June 18, 2003

The sign on the side of the hangar said "Tropical Fighters." Inside sat an old jet fighter plane. It was tiny, and the cockpit didn't seem big enough for a human being.

"That doesn't look like anything Dad ever flew as a test pilot," Carolyn said.

Steve Holmstrom greeted us warmly. He looked about thirty years old, medium-tall, with short brown hair and a tan, handsome face.

Leading us into an air-conditioned office, he said, "Ed's out of town, and I'm taking care of his dog." A gangly German shepherd puppy danced around Steve's legs.

"We'd like to take you to lunch, as I promised on the phone," I said. "Anywhere you say."

"What kind of food do you like?" Steve bent down to put a leash on the dog. "There are plenty of places around here."

"Anywhere, as long as it's air-conditioned," Carolyn said.

"Let me take this dog out for a minute and then I can leave," Steve said.

While we waited, we looked around the office. There were shelves with caps and T-shirts for sale, lounge chairs, a couple of desks, and an array of framed certificates and licenses on the walls.

One photo of a fighter plane bore the scrawled inscription, "Ed Eraser: Next time I'll fly with you, not against you!" It was signed, "Yuri."

We agreed on seafood at the Key Colony Club, in a small community off the main road near our Holiday Inn. Steve ordered the conch (pronounced "conk"). But both he and the waitress warned us that it was an acquired taste; we might just like to try a bit of his while we enjoyed something more familiar. Carolyn and I ordered shrimp salads.

While we waited for the food, Steve began to talk about what he remembered about July 31, 2001.

"Unfortunately, I was working in the maintenance shop when it happened. Didn't see him take off. I'd met and talked to your brother a few times before that day, but I didn't know him well."

"Ed called me into the office right away, because they thought there might be something mechanically wrong with the plane. They had me listen in on the radio in case the pilot needed instructions. Sometimes a customer has trouble getting their landing gear down. So I can say, 'try this, try that.' But he was speaking so little on the radio, we didn't know what the problem was. At first."

"Do you remember what Milo said?"

"By the time I got on the radio, he was coming in to land. He said something like, 'This doesn't look good. I'm going to go back around.' And he was coming in fine. So he went back around again, and on approach he said, 'No, no, I can't do it.' And then he stopped responding on the radio and just flew away.

"There were a couple of other pilots on the field who jumped in their planes and went up to look for him. The guy that owns the biplane was already in the air, so we contacted him. They all went around looking but they never found him. They didn't know which direction the Cessna had gone. We assumed he was circling the area. The last thing anybody does if they're upset or frightened is head out over the water."

"That makes sense."

"The Coast Guard finally found him, way past Key West. The Navy planes took it from there. They followed him all the way to the Cuban air space. They were flying alongside him, and they could see him in the cockpit. But they said that he wouldn't look over at them."

"How could he *not* look at them?" I said. "Jet fighter planes?"

"One person said that he was slumped over the controls, and, of course, we immediately thought something had happened to him, physically. But then, when they got back on the ground, another person said that he wasn't slumped, but *hunched* over the controls, and he was making an absolute beeline for Havana.

"When we heard this, we assumed he was defecting or something, and we realized that there was more to it than just a student pilot panicking. What he actually did – going to Cuba – would have been the last thing we expected."

"And then, afterwards," I asked, "did you have a visit from a man named Anthony Russo, from the F.B.I. office in Key West?"

"Yes, he came here and went upstairs and talked to Ed. I've spoken to him a few times since then."

"Have you?"

"Yes. Most recently yesterday. After we got the fax."

"What fax?"

"The one Milo's brother-in-law sent us. It warned that Milo was in the area again. Milo's wife also called here and told us that they were sending that same fax to the F.A.A. and to all airports in Southern Florida.

"But I found out recently that she'd notified flight schools and the F.A.A. in this area when he *first* came here, two years ago. I wasn't aware of it, but the F.B.I. said that the airport manager had received a copy of that and had given it to the flight school where Milo was flying at the time, down at the other end of the airport."

"Grant Air Services?"

"Yes, but *we* never got that fax. The airport manager at the time seemed to favor Grant Air. I don't know if it was political or what, but she never let us know about it. If we had received that fax, this whole thing could have been prevented."

"I'd like to know more about the note they found in his car the day after this happened." I nodded to the young man who was filling my coffee cup.

"I never got to see the note, but I was there when they came and got the car. They wanted one of us to be out there before they took it away. They had cordoned off the area. All I know about the note was what I read in the newspaper articles."

"I see."

"Apparently, there were maps and charts of Cuba, and navigation books." Steve took a sip of his Diet Coke. "When they brought your brother back to Miami, he was saying that he'd just panicked and that's why he ended up there. But when the police searched the car, they found the irrefutable evidence. Apparently there was something in the car. A note about Cuba or Castro or something."

The waitress stopped at our table. To Steve, she said, "You've been talking. I love that in a man! Have you ladies tried the conch?"

"We each had some, thank you. You were right; it's an acquired taste."

A few minutes later, Carolyn asked, "Did Milo fly around the airport quite a few times before he took off for Cuba?"

"Well, normally on a solo, Ed would have the student take off and fly around the airport pattern three times, to see how they did," Steve said. "I think he did the fly-by the first time, and then he was coming back around and just veered off. It couldn't have taken more than ten minutes. And it was probably another five minutes before Ed realized something was wrong.

"It's not unusual; the first time someone comes in by themselves, they're a little leery. And if the winds aren't perfect, and it doesn't feel perfect, then they do another go-around. I think that it was more his tone of voice than the words he used that alarmed us."

"Ed Steigerwald's been doing this awhile, hasn't he?" I asked Steve.

"He's been flying for twenty-eight years."

"Does a Cessna 172 have two seats or four?"

"It's a four-seater. A pretty common airplane for training."

"Before this happened," Carolyn asked, "Ed was pretty confident that Milo could do this, right?"

"Yes, he said that he exhibited a lot of skill with flying. Your father was a pilot. Your brother probably flew with him, too, didn't he?"

"From the time he was small," I answered. "As often as Dad would take him."

"We have family pictures of the three of us sitting on the wing of a plane," Carolyn said. "Milo was still in diapers."

"Most student pilots wouldn't be capable of doing what he did," Steve said. "So he had to have been studying and planning it, planning the heading. It would be easy to miss an island from ninety miles away if he was even a few degrees off course."

"So, even if he were more experienced than he let on," I asked, "he would not have been able to hit Cuba without some kind of planning?"

"Right," Steve nodded. "I myself have about two hundred hours of flying, and I don't know that I could navigate without extensive preparation."

"In the note he left in his car, did Milo mention that he wanted to *kidnap* Fidel Castro?"

"That's what I read in the newspaper. He said Cuba was an oppressive culture or government, or something like that, and he was going to try to kidnap Castro."

"Milo told me he worked with some Cuban garbage men on his other job – besides Pizza Hut," I said. "He said they talked about their country a lot. But they wouldn't talk about their government. So perhaps Milo made the leap ..."

"From the Cubans I know, that's the case," Steve said. "They love their country. One of the ministers from our church went on a mission down there last year. He said it was an absolutely wonderful country and that the people are basically happy, but they're not happy with their government.

"U.S. citizens can't go to Cuba unless they're hosted. They're really cracking down. But I guess you can still go to Cuba if you fly through Mexico or South America.

"There's a yearly regatta," Steve went on, "from Key West to Havana. The I.N.S. and some other federal agencies held a briefing at the pre-race meeting this year. Then, when the participants came back, their vessels were boarded and the authorities took whatever knickknacks they'd collected. I don't know if they were trying to seize the boats or what. If you take your boat into Cuba, it's like exporting it from the United States, or something like that. There has been a big stink about this in the papers lately."

"How many lessons did Milo have before his solo flight?" I drained my cup.

"I don't know, but he'd been flying with us for weeks. When Ed was confident that John – we knew him as John – could do it, he let him go up alone."

"In one of the newspaper accounts, Milo had offered to take a friend up in the plane."

"Ed would never let him do that."

"What was the weather like that day? July 31, 2001?"

"I don't remember there being any bad weather that day," Steve responded. "The Keys stay pretty dry, and if there is weather, it's over in five minutes. I don't remember anyone having any concerns about whether John was flying near any thunderstorms or anything like that. That would have been one of the first things we'd consider."

"How long did it take Milo to get to Cuba?"

"I don't remember because time was, like, crawling. Then the Coast Guard told us that he'd landed near Havana. On a beach. He had crashed, and we were worried about that. It wasn't until the TV news that we actually found out anything for sure."

The waitress returned to refill our coffee. "Anyone for dessert?"

We all passed, until she said, "We have great Key lime pie!"

"Okay!" Carolyn and I decided to split a piece.

"Milo said that the Cubans treated him well. That they put him up in a luxury hotel."

"Well, everyone's usually running the other way. Not trying to get into Cuba, but trying to get *out*."

"That's true. Yes!" We laughed.

"He came back with some Communist literature under his arm," I said.

Steve nodded. "Quite an adventure, I'll bet. You know, I wasn't sure how the Cubans were going to handle that. It was up in the air for several days."

"So to speak," I mused. "I can't understand how he escaped being shot down – by our planes or theirs."

"Probably post-9-11, he would have."

"Did you have any 'other people' learning to fly in the Keys at that time? During that summer? You know, before 9-11?"

Steve read my mind. "That was up north, at Huffman Aviation. In fact, I was at an aircraft inspector's class when 9-11 happened, with a guy that worked at Huffman."

"Can you see Cuba from the end of the Keys?" Carolyn asked.

"You mean, could he have flown with visual flight rules? No. And I think that there's very little chance for someone to just take off and head for whatever direction they think is Cuba, randomly, and being able to make it. No, you wouldn't be able to see it until you were halfway there. Then, you couldn't see the land behind you, so you'd be navigating over open water. There are no points of reference. It's not like following the coast. I could find Miami from here, flying over land, without planning it, but …"

"How long before Milo's plane would have run out of gas?"

"I remember we were talking about that while we were waiting that day. We were trying to estimate how full the tanks were, because Ed had gone up with him a few times before he soloed, just to make sure things were okay. But even with half-tanks, he would have had an hour or so, or a couple hours worth of fuel, or even more.

"The plane burns about ten gallons an hour, and it holds sixty gallons. So, even at half-tanks, that's three hours till bone dry. I don't remember whether we determined that it had been filled right before or not, but they usually top off before they go."

"Were there life jackets, in case he had to ditch?"

"Yeah, we have to keep life jackets on board. And there's an emergency locator in the airplane – in all airplanes, actually. It's a little beacon just like they have on boats. They call it an E.L.T. on airplanes – Emergency Locator Transmitter. It has a little G-switch that sets it off."

"Can a plane like that easily make the trip to Cuba?"

"Oh yes. Most planes like that can easily go between six hundred and a thousand miles, no problem. The longest range of single-engine piston planes is about twelve hundred miles. That's for the bigger single-engine ones."

"So these Cessna 172s have two tanks, one on each side?"

"Yes, but they gravity feed together."

"What did this plane look like?"

"I can show you one when we get back to the hangar. There's one on the other side of our building that looks very similar to the one your brother flew. You can take a picture of it, if you like."

"In the car on the way over here, you mentioned a phone message. One Milo left recently."

"Well, I got a call from Paradise Aviation. They told me that there was a message for Ed, so I went over and listened to it, and it was him saying, 'Hi, this is John Reese, the one who stole your plane and cracked it up in Cuba.'

"Then he said, 'If I was a real man, I'd make good on it, but I guess we both know I'm never going to be able to pay you for it.' Or something like that. He started to say something else, but he stopped and hung up in mid-sentence. It was like he was starting to express a thought and then, click.

"Actually, there were two calls. He called once and left a message on the answering machine, and that's the one I heard, and then there was another where he spoke to Leslie over in the Paradise office. She works the front desk. I think she's working today. I don't know whether she's willing to talk to you or not."

"Thanks," I said, "We'll try …"

"Maybe he called because he was planning to come back down here," Carolyn said.

"I think it was last Wednesday that we got that phone message."

"That was the same day Milo called *me*, in Santa Barbara," I said. "He sounded very strange."

~~~

During manic episodes, patients feel excessively high and full of energy, and their thoughts go a mile a minute. They may go for days with no sleep, have grandiose ideas and believe they have special powers or insights. They often have problems with judgment and impulse control and end up doing things that have major consequences – bankruptcy, divorce or arrest.

– Husseini K. Manji, M.D., director of the Mood and Anxiety Disorders Program of the National Institute for Mental Health

As the combination of euphoric mood and mental quickness develops, the manic individual begins to feel tremendously self-confident, even fearless. This is the so-called grandiosity of the manic state. Fears of unpleasant consequences disappear altogether, and reckless enthusiasm takes over. The affected person may seek out new adventures and experiences with no regard for the possible adverse repercussions.
  – *Bipolar Disorder: A Guide for Patients and Families*, by Francis Mark Mondimore, M.D., Johns Hopkins University Press, 1999, p.12

Chapter Forty-Two: Marathon to Key West

While Carolyn copied news clippings from Steve's files, I went next door. The girl at the Paradise Air desk told me that Leslie was out to lunch, but she said I could talk to the present owner, Ms. Collins.

"Hello," said a voice from behind us. "I'm Carol Collins. May I help you?"

I introduced myself to a slim, attractive, dark-haired woman. The polo shirt tucked into khaki slacks said "Aviation for Women" on the pocket.

"I wasn't here the day of his solo," Carol said, "but I gave Mr. Reese his first introductory flight."

"Would you be willing to answer a few questions?" I asked.

"Sure. Come on up to my office."

The windowless space upstairs was painted light green, with a tasteful dark wooden desk and matching bookcases. On the wall was a framed award naming Carol Collins "Flight Instructor of the Year, Miami District."

"It was interesting, in light of what we learned later." Carol motioned me into a chair across from hers. "Your brother was congenial and enthusiastic. He pretended to be a novice who had never flown before, acting as if everything was new and exciting. He said that his – your – father was a pilot and that he, John, as he called himself, had always wanted to learn to fly."

We talked about her purchase of Paradise Aviation.

"When this incident with your brother occurred, it hurt the business financially and politically. The competition jumped on this and said we were dangerous. I thought Ed was joking when he said, 'I'm not flying anymore.' But your brother was his last student pilot.

"You know, as a flight instructor, you're always putting your heart into your students. When they solo, you're there on the ground thinking, are they in trouble? What are they doing? And then, when this happened, when Ed realized he'd been taken advantage of, he was depressed about it."

"The plane was insured, right?"

"Ed only got reimbursed a small amount," Carol said. "Fifteen thousand dollars. The plane was worth sixty. And this business runs on a five-percent margin. The insurance company said the plane was not insured for when it was out of the country.

"Of course, we told them that we didn't *authorize* it to be out of the country, that we didn't *plan* for it to be out of the country. But that's all they paid."

"So it really hurt."

"I'm afraid so. And then everyone, including the F.B.I., asked us whether we could have seen this coming."

The phone rang. I motioned for her to take the call. She was discussing the insurance premium on a new Cessna. Twenty thousand dollars a year.

After she hung up, I said, "I wanted to find out about the phone message that Milo left here last week."

"Yes. He said he was sorry, but somebody had to do something about Castro. There was no way he could repay the cost of the airplane. And then he said something about wanting to come down here to apologize in person."

"And now he might be doing just that."

"Yes, I guess so."

"I appreciate your time," I said as we parted. "Good luck with your new business."

I went back to find Carolyn. After picking out a shirt with the Tropical Fighters logo to take home to Ted, we thanked Steve again.

We drove south, past more marinas, elegant houses, docks. Even the *in*elegant houses had docks. They were more common than garages. We went through Bahia Honda Key, Big Pine Key, No Name Key, Saddlebunch Keys, Big Coppit Key. Signs warned of deer as we drove through a wildlife sanctuary. Deer?

We arrived in the town of Key West to the typical traffic problems of any small city. "Welcome to the Conch Republic," Carolyn read out of the tourist leaflet that she'd picked up at the hotel.

"Isn't this where they have the Ernest Hemingway look-alike contest?"

"I think so. Maybe we'll get some tips on writing."

"Or maybe one of the winners will buy us a drink."

A jet flew overhead. "This is where they have the Naval Air Station," I said. "Remember those Navy jets that followed Milo? They came from here."

As we walked around the harbor, Diet Cokes on ice provided only some relief from the heat. I got out my cell phone and rummaged through my purse for Anthony Russo's phone number. He was the F.B.I. officer who had investigated Milo's case.

When I finally got hold of him, Mr. Russo was not willing to talk about Milo's case. He did give me the phone number of the man in the Miami F.B.I. office who could tell me how to get copies of the file under the Freedom of Information and Privacy Act.

The "Privacy" part meant that I would have to get my brother's notarized signature before I could make the request. I guessed there was slim chance of that.

After that, changing roles from female sleuths to everyday tourists, we indeed saw the sights of Key West, at least as much as we could see on the harbor walk. We had our picture taken at Land's End (three hours *before* sunset), and I photographed Carolyn in front of a fancy hotel on the marina. At about five, we decided to head back to Marathon. It took us awhile to get out of town. Key West has a rush hour.

June 19, 2003

Before breakfast, I checked the messages on my cell phone. Dad had some news. Carolyn and I looked at each other warily as I punched in his number.

"Milo turned himself in to the Fort Lauderdale police yesterday."

"Fort Lauderdale?"

"Yeah, it's just north of Miami. I guess, when Miami didn't want him, he went there. I'll give you the phone number."

I called the Fort Lauderdale Police Department. Yes, they had Milo John Reese, and they would be transferring him to the Federal Detention Center in Miami. They would not give me any other details.

We visited the air-conditioned workout room at the Holiday Inn, then took cooling showers.

Driving back through Crawl Key, Grassy Key, Conch Key, we decided to come back someday. In the winter.

Carolyn took out one of the photocopies she had made in Steve's office. In addition to news articles there was a letter from Milo.

"I'll read it to you," she said. "It's dated February, 2002. He must have written it right around the time he was released from the detention center in Miami."

Dear Ed,

    This is a long overdue letter. I told a judge in court last Thursday that I stole the Cessna. The F.B.I. already knows I'm guilty – I left a note in my car stating that I was going to try to kidnap Fidel Castro. We planned this for 1½ years. I'm sorry it had to be your plane.

"We?" I was incredulous. Carolyn went on reading.

You're a great guy and I respect you also as a pilot. If I said I was sorry about everything, *that would not be entirely factual. Castro is a cruel dictator, and I'm glad I at least tried. I'm probably going to do some time – maybe a lot. I hope I can go to a camp and work.*
    If I can ever earn enough money I'm going to pay you back for the Cessna.

"It's signed, '*Respectfully, John Reese.*'"

~~~

Shame affects not only the mentally ill, but also those living with the afflicted. Recent studies reflect the notion that the foundation of shame involves the awareness of not living up to one's own [if convoluted] code of standards, rules, or norms or those of others.
    – From *New Hope for People with Bipolar Disorder*, by Jan Fawcett, M.D., Bernard Golden, Ph.D., and Nancy Rosenfeld; copyright 2000 by Jan Fawcett, Bernard Golden, and Nancy Rosenfeld. Used by permission of Prima Publishing, a division of Random House, Inc.

Part Ten:

Consequences

Why has government been instituted at all? Because the passions of men will not conform to the dictates of reason and justice, without constraint.

— Alexander Hamilton, *The Federalist* (1787-1788)

Other personality traits seen in bipolar disorders...include a rebellious streak that seems to bring the person into deliberate conflict with authority figures and reckless behavior based on grandiose thinking.
　　　– Adult Bipolar Disorders: Understanding Your Diagnosis & Getting help, by Mitzi Waltz, O'Reilly & Associates, Inc., 2002, p. 46

Chapter Forty-Three: Insights

August 26, 2003

　　I arrived at the Federal Office on Liberty Street in downtown Reno. Although it was a warm afternoon, I could see signs of fall in the few trees that lined the streets in this part of town. In my briefcase was my brother's signed permission to speak with his public defender in Nevada. His name was Michael Powell.

　　Powell greeted me in jeans and cowboy boots. His slightly graying hair was tied in a pony tail, and his smile put me at ease. Milo would probably have liked him.

　　I soon learned that Powell was familiar, as was Celeste Higgins in Miami, with bipolar disorder. He, also, had represented many people afflicted with mental illness.

In his experience, he said, "Mania causes extreme self-confidence. The chemical process in the brain leads to high-risk behavior and poor choices. Bipolar people don't obey the rules because they think they know better: 'I think, therefore it's right.' Then they get into trouble."

Powell said, "It was understandable that Milo might have had trouble staying at the halfway house. That place has a lot of rules."

We talked about what had happened after Milo broke his parole two months before. When asked why he had flown back to Miami, Milo had hedged.

"He told everyone a different story – his wife, his parole officer, his counselor, me," Powell said. "He doesn't know exactly what people want to hear, so he tries different things.

"But when he got before the judge, he told *another* version. He said that he had been inappropriately touched by his therapist. I yelled at him afterwards. I said to him, 'There's one thing you never do. You never say anything in court that you haven't yet told your attorney!'"

The judge instructed the probation department to investigate, and they subsequently found nothing to substantiate Milo's accusation. Milo then asked the judge why his therapist had not been fired, and the judge reminded him that they would not fire someone on Milo's word alone.

"Normally, breaking parole involves being sent back to prison," Mr. Powell continued, "but Milo's parole officer liked him, and she convinced the judge to allow him to go back to the halfway house and extend the time by six months. The judge had agreed that John would be better off having access to local mental health resources. The halfway house has a 'pill watch.' John volunteered to be monitored with regular blood tests to show whether or not he was taking his medication."

The more efficient option, and one that would have meant Milo would be free sooner, Powell said, might have been for him to accept a four-month prison term. This would involve *no* supervised release afterward. However, Nevada does not have a federal detention center, and his stay would be contracted out to the Reno state prison, where they probably would not let him have his medication. Powell finally decided that this was a bad choice for Milo at that time.

Michael Powell had warned Milo that he could no longer work three jobs, as he had been doing before he left for Florida in June.

"This causes stress, and it interferes with the meds," Powell told him. "And you can't do everything just because it pops into you head. Next time you get an idea, call me first!"

After returning to the halfway house for a few weeks, and getting a job delivering Diners Club meals, Milo called his parole officer. He said that he wanted to go home to his wife's apartment because he was not sleeping.

"The parole officer agreed to his request," said Mr. Powell. "When he went to Mental Health the next day for his blood test, the doctors realized he was not well, and they committed him to their hospital facility on a seventy-two-hour hold. Apparently, they thought he was cycling down into a depressed state, and they wanted to keep him for observation."

"They were afraid he would try to commit suicide?" I half-said, half-asked.

Powell raised his shoulders and slowly nodded his head.

I asked Mr. Powell if he'd seen Milo lately.

"Not for several weeks," he said, "because my role in this ended after the court appearance."

"Well," I offered, "we never know what Milo will do next. You may be representing him again."

And while we spoke that day, as I later learned, Milo was breaking the terms of his parole once again. At that very moment, he was aboard another plane to Miami, in search of yet another windmill of madness.

~~~

Depressives use the phrase 'over the edge' all the time to delineate the passage from pain to madness. This very physical description

frequently entails falling "into the abyss."... Few of us have ever fallen off the edge of anything, and certainly not into an abyss ... When asked, people describe the abyss pretty consistently. In the first place, it's dark. You are falling away from the sunlight toward a place where the shadows are black. Inside it, you cannot see, and the dangers are everywhere ... While you are falling, you don't know how deep you can go, or whether you can in any way stop yourself. You hit invisible things over and over again until you are shredded, and yet your environment is too unstable for you to catch onto anything.
– *The Noonday Demon: An Atlas of Depression*, by Andrew Solomon, Scribner, 2001, paperback edition 2003, p. 27

At midyear 1998, an estimated 283,800 mentally ill offenders were incarcerated in the nations's prisons and jails. In recent surveys completed by the Bureau of Justice Statistics, 16 percent of those in local jails reported either a mental condition or an overnight stay in a mental hospital.
– Bureau of Justice Statistics Special Report: Mental Health and Treatment of Inmates and Probationers, by Paula M. Ditton, Bureau of Justice Statistician, July 1999, http://www.ojp.usdoj.gov/bjs/

Chapter Forty-Four: The Visit

February 12, 2004

When I got back from my walk, I checked my messages. "Call Bop," were Dad's only words. Oh God, I thought, who died? At eighty-nine, my father was the youngest of four children, one ten years older than he.

I dialed the number. "Hello?"

"Hi, Dad. What's up?"

"I found out they're sending Milo to Lompoc. Would you call the prison to see if he's there yet?"

My brother had been "in transit" to the federal prison at Lompoc from Reno for the past six weeks. We'd learned that federal prisoners who are transferred from one place to another go through a distribution center in Oklahoma City. Sometimes it takes time for them to be routed onto a flight to their specific destination.

Dad gave me the phone number of the prison. "Would you also talk to someone on the medical staff about this new M.R.I. treatment? I know it's a long shot, but ..."

He had mentioned this during every phone call for the past three weeks.

"Dad, that treatment is still in the experimental stages. We're lucky if they're giving Milo any medication at all, let alone a procedure so new that it hasn't even been approved by the F.D.A. yet."

Dad was still clutching at shadows of hope. In a kind of manic state himself recently, my father had even tried to make me promise that I would *personally* see that medical science found a cure for bipolar disorder. I'd reminded him that I was not a physician or a clinical psychologist.

February 16, 2004

The Federal Correctional Facility in Lompoc, California, is at the top of a gentle rise outside of town above a valley rich in farmland and famous for its flowers.

We had called the prison and learned that nothing would be allowed in except for picture I.D. There were clothing restrictions: We could wear nothing provocative, nothing beige. We could bring up to $20 each for the vending machines, but any money given to prisoners must be in the form of a money order, and it must come through the mail.

In the entry of the main lobby, Ted and I walked across the large mat with the Great Seal of the United States. Lining the walls were photos of President Bush, John Ashcroft, and other government officials. A husky young man in uniform asked if he could help. We told him we had come from Santa Barbara to see my brother, Milo John Reese. A young, dark-haired woman behind the desk typed the name into the computer.

"Yes, you can probably see him," she said. "It will be just a few minutes."

We took off our shoes, belts, watches, and rings and watched them disappear on the conveyor belt. Officials in uniform motioned for us to walk through the x-ray arch. I went first, with no problem, but Ted set off an alarm. Finally, he and the guard figured out that it was the dental plate in his mouth. We filled out forms, checking "No" to carrying items such as firearms, explosives, narcotics, dynamite, and sharp implements. Then we offered the backs of our hands to be stamped.

Our escort made small talk as he led us through a door to a long hallway. His name was Daniel, and the sleeves of his uniform bulged with muscle. On the walls were photos of employees and a large board with their nametags and schedules. He said that we were lucky we hadn't come yesterday or the day before. It was Valentine's Day weekend, and they'd had record-breaking crowds.

As we held our hands under the ultraviolet lamp, a person behind the window scrutinized them and motioned us forward.

At the end of the outside walkway was a low building with concrete picnic tables outside. As Daniel unlocked the gate, I looked at the people inside the chain link fence and realized why the clothing restrictions excluded beige. The inmates were easily spotted in their khaki-colored shirts and slacks.

"You might have to sit with him outside," Daniel said. "It's pretty crowded indoors on a day like today." I shivered in the cold wind.

Daniel held the door open for us as we entered a large visiting room. At the central desk, he handed our papers to another guard behind the counter, who typed Milo's name into his computer.

"They're paging him now. It should be just about ten minutes," he said, over the din of noise.

As we waited for Milo, I tried to look nonchalant as I snuck glances at the faces around us. Over by the window sat a heavily tattooed young inmate talking to a teenage girl in a sweatshirt. On her lap was a screaming infant. Behind us stood a whole family of people dressed as if for church. One woman wore Victorian-style heels, a flowered skirt, and a fuzzy fake fur coat. Her banana curls turned from black to orange as they dangled down over her ears.

An inmate came in accompanied by three teenage boys. They duck-walked through the door in their extra-long baggy jeans.

With his hands on the shoulders of two of them, the man turned his head back and forth, talking quietly into each of their ears.

Another family was clustered near us, around the desk, waiting. A small girl, dressed in red, with her black hair in multiple braids, was looking through one of the books from the round table nearby. She was following the words with her finger, but skipping around and going far too fast to be reading. I learned her name was Alexandra.

"Alexandra, how old are you?" I asked.

"Five."

"Do you like to read?"

"My daddy will read me this today," she said with a smile that squeezed my heart.

I spied a round table nearby and quickly collected three odd chairs from different families of visitors by asking their permission in my most polite voice. After we had staked out our space, Ted waited while I went to enter my dollar in the vending machine outside. I pressed assorted buttons and received a large, strong cup of coffee with unwanted cream and sugar. As it turned out, it would be my lunch that day.

When I returned inside, Milo was sitting with Ted. He stood up to give me a hug, and I realized, as I did each time I saw him, just how tall he was. His receding hair was peppered with gray, and he looked older. But even though the whites of his eyes were bloodshot, the pupils were still the same fierce blue.

"How are you, Milo?"

"Great."

"How do you like it here? Are they treating you well?"

"I like it. There's always a lot to do. Unlike Oklahoma. This place has a library, TVs, a room with typewriters …"

Typewriters, I thought to myself. *That's usually how it starts with Milo.*

"How's the food?"

"Good. Today, for lunch, we had polish sausage, chicken, mashed potatoes, and ice cream. I've got to start watching it. Probably put on weight just since I got here."

"Can you work out? Is there a gym?"

"Yeah, but I like running around the track."

"That's good exercise."

"What about medication?"

"They're giving me lithium twice a day."

"Any side effects, Milo?"

"It makes me kind of tired, that's all."

We talked for almost two hours. Ted's lunch was a double pack of oatmeal cookies and a Coke, also from the vending machine. We reminisced about the ranch, about fun times in the past, about some of Dad's flying stories.

Milo asked about Ted's family. I realized that, except for the setting, we were having a normal conversation. There were some things I wanted to ask Milo, but I didn't. Had he learned the ultimate lesson about taking his medication? Was he ever going to face up to the responsibility of his illness?

I did ask about the letter he had sent Dad from Cuba. "You wrote a return address of 'Great Hotel, Havana, Cuba.' Do you remember the hotel's real name?"

"Hotel Isabel," he answered.

"So you get out of here on the third of March, huh?"

"Yeah. They'll give me a bus ticket back to Reno. Then I'll have seventeen months of supervised release. I'll have to report to a parole officer once a month."

"What are you planning to do when you get back to Reno?"

"I'll get a job where I only have to work six hours a day and make great tips."

"And what job is that, Milo?" Ted asked.

"Delivering pizza, of course."

That night, at home, I looked in the Cuba travel guide. Hotel Isabel was listed, and it was under the heading "Top End." Milo had indeed traveled first-class.

~~~

Offenders between ages 45 and 54 were the most likely to be identified as mentally ill … About 20 percent of state prisoners, 10 percent of federal prisoners, 23 percent of jail inmates, and

21 percent of probationers between ages 45 and 54 had a mental illness, compared to 14 percent of state inmates, 7 percent of federal inmates, 13 percent of jail inmates, and 14 percent of probationers age 24 or younger.
– Bureau of Justice Statistics Special Report: Mental Health and Treatment of Inmates and Probationers, by Paula M. Ditton, Bureau of Justice Statistician, July 1999, http://www.ojp.usdoj.gov/bjs

"You are old, Father William," the young man said,
"And your hair has become very white;
And yet you incessantly stand on your head—
Do you think, at your age, it is right?"

—*You are old, Father William*, Lewis Carroll

Epilogue

July 20, 2004

"Hi, Cynthia. This is Milo."

"Hi, where are you?"

"I'm in Reno. Back at the halfway house."

"How are you doing?"

"Fine. Got my old job back."

"Let me guess. Delivering pizza."

"You got it."

"Are they giving you your meds?"

"Yeah. Say, did you stay at the Holiday Marina Hotel when you were in Miami?"

"Uh, yes. How did *you* know?"

"I was there, too. I saw you getting out of a cab."

"You *what*?"

"It was raining."

"Why, yes. That was the second day we were there. Carolyn and I got caught in a thunderstorm. But why didn't you come in and see us? We were looking all over Miami for you!"

"I wasn't sure it was you …"

"Well, why didn't you go ask at the front desk, for God's sakes?"

"Did you go over to that Bayshore Marketplace?"

"That's where we looked the first day. We had lunch there. We thought you liked that place. Free samples at the food fair …"

"Dad said you talked to Celeste Higgins."

"Yes. She was very nice to us."

"I had a crush on her."

"Oh, really …?"

"Yeah. But she missed her chance with me ..."

"Very funny, Milo. You're still your old, charming self. Your eternally *young*, charming self."

"I think the phone card is out of ..."

I recently came across a note I had written to myself shortly after he was released from prison the first time:

List of Things to Tell Milo's Parole Officer:

– Milo will answer "yes," "fine," or "you bet" to any question you pose. Then, he'll change the subject.
– He will take his medications for awhile. But only for awhile.
– And he will get sick. Again.
– And he will leave. Again.
– And nothing will stop him.
– For the past forty years, this has been his pattern.
– And, yes, Milo is crazy. Like a fox.

Three years after he flew to Cuba, Milo sent me this letter:

September 2004
Dear Cynthia,

I don't take my medication because I want *the experience of mania, so I can return to all the excitement an episode has to offer. I remember thinking, the first time I arrived in Key West, "This is Paradise." This may explain why I returned to the place of my dramatic flight, The Florida Keys.*

I have a fear of death that haunts me occasionally. When I'm manic, I feel very close to God. And I have assurance that, if I die, I'll go to Heaven. Before I took off for Cuba, I felt there was a good chance I would not survive, but I would be forever OK nevertheless.

When I'm depressed I feel insignificant, without a future.
Love, Milo

It is now the summer of 2005. Two weeks ago, Milo violated his supervised release for the third time. He quit his job without telling his parole officer, then left the halfway house and went to a small local airport to inquire about flying lessons. Next, he tried, without success, to buy an airline ticket to Florida. Perhaps by this time he was on the "no fly" list.

Milo was finally picked up in downtown Reno for disturbing the peace. When he appeared in court several days later, he lost his temper in front of the judge.

At present, Milo is on his way to another federal prison. We are told that this one has a mental facility, and we hope this means he will receive medication. At least he will have three meals a day and a place to sleep for the next ten months.

Letter to a Small Spot of Sanity

I hope you hear me
Wherever you are
I hope you find
That small part of you
Making true sense of things
Is it there
Beneath the murky
Depths of madness
Under the shroud of denial
Tucked away in the creases
Between changes of mind?
Or is it, after all, with the stars
In perception's manic heights?
Should we without wings
Look inside ourselves
For instruments of abandon
With which to soar
Along with you?

– Cynthia Martin, 2004

Bibliography

A Brilliant Madness: Living with Manic-Depressive Illness, by Patty Duke & Gloria Hochman, Bantam Books, 1992.

Adult Bipolar Disorders: Understanding Your Diagnosis & Getting Help, by Mitzi Waltz, O'Reilly Media, Inc., 2002.

A Mood Apart: The Thinker's Guide to Emotion and its Disorders, by Peter C. Whybrow, M.D., HarperPerrenial, A Division of HarperCollins Publishers, by arrangement with Perseus Basic Books, 1997.

An Unquiet Mind: A Memoir of Moods and Madness, by Kay Redfield Jamison, Vintage Books, A Division of Random House, Inc., New York, 1996.

A Primer on Mental Disorders: a Guide for Educators, Families, and Students, Thomas E. Allen, M.D., Mayer C. Liebman, M.D., Lee Crandall Park, M.D., & William C. Wimmer, M.D., Scarecrow Press, www.scarecrowpress.com 2001.

Bipolar Disorder: A Guide for Patients and Families, by Francis Mark Mondimore, M.D., Johns Hopkins University Press, 1999.

Bipolar Disorder Demystified: Mastering the Tightrope of Manic Depression, by Lana R. Castle, Marlowe & Co., an Imprint of Avalon Publishing Group Inc., New York, 2003.

Brothel: Mustang Ranch and Its Women, by Alexa Albert, M.D., Ballantine Books, 2001.

Bureau of Justice Statistics Special Report: Mental Health and Treatment of Inmates and Probationers, by Paula M. Ditton,

Bureau of Justice Statistician, July 1999, http://www.ojp.usdoj.gov/bjs

Coping with Bipolar Disorder: A Guide to Living with Manic Depression, by Steven Jones, Peter Hayward, Dominic Lam, Oneworld Publications, 2002.

Criminalizing the Seriously Mentally Ill: The Abuse of Jails as Mental Hospitals, by Torrey, Stieber, Ezediel, Wolfe, Sharfstein, Noble, Flynn, a joint report of the National for the Mentally Ill and Public Citizen's Health Research Group, 1992.

Depression and Bipolar Disorders, by Virginia Edwards, Your Personal Health Series, Firefly Books (U.S.) Inc., 2002. Reprinted with permission of Key Porter Books. Copyright © by Virginia Edwards.

Electroboy: A Memoir of Mania, by Andy Behrman, Random House Trade Paperbacks, 2002.

Genetics and Mental Illness: Evolving Issues for Research and Society, Edited by Laura Lee Hall, National Alliance for the Mentally Ill, Arlington, Virginia, Plenum Press, New York and London, 1996.

I Am Not Sick I Don't Need Help, Xavier Amador, Ph.D., and Anna-Lica Johanson, Ph.D., Vida Press, 2000

Out of the Shadows, by E. Fuller Torrey, M.D., John Wiley and Sons, Inc., 1997.

Peter Pan, by J.M. Barrie, reprinted with the permission of Atheneum Books for Young Readers, an imprint of Simon & Schuster Children's Publishing Division, Copyright 1911, Charles Scribner's Sons; Copyright 1939 Lady Cynthia Asquith and Peter Llewlyn Davies.

National Institute of Mental Health Information Resources and Inquiries: 6001 Executive Boulevard, Room 8184, MSC 9663, Bethesda, MD 20892-9663, toll-free at 886-615-6464. Publications may be ordered online at http://www.nimh.nih.gov

New Hope for Bipolar Disorder, by Jan Fawcett, M.D., Bernard Golden, Ph.D., and Nancy Rosenfeld, Prima Publishing, 2000.

The Invisible Plague: The Rise of Mental Illness from 1750 to the Present, by E. Fuller Torrey, M.D. and Judy Miller, Rutgers University Press, 2002 .

Surviving Manic Depression, by E. Fuller Torrey, M.D. & Michael B. Knable, D.O., Basic Books, 2002.

The Alchemist, by Paulo Coelho, translated by Alan R. Clarke, HarperSanFrancisco, A Division of HarperCollins *Publishers*, 1993.

The Bipolar Disorder Survival Guide, David J. Miklowitz, PhD, The Guilford Press, New York/London, 2002.

The Burden of Sympathy: How Families Cope with Mental Illness, David A. Karp, Oxford University Press, 2001.

The Noonday Demon: An Atlas of Depression, Andrew Solomon, Scribner, 2003.

The Problem of the Puer Aeternus, Marie-Louise von Franz (1915-1998), edited by Daryl Sharp, Inner City Books, Copyright 2000.

The Skipping Stone: Ripple Effects of Mental Illness on the Family, Mona Wasow, Clinical Professor, Science & Behavior Books, Inc., Palo Alto, CA, 1995.

Taming Bipolar Disorder, A Psychology Today *Here to Help* book, Lori Oliwenstein, Alpha Books, published by the Penguin Group, 2004.

Touched with Fire: Manic Depressive Illness and the Artistic Temperament, by Kay Redfield Jamison, Copyright 1993. Reprinted with the permission of The Free Press, a division of Simon & Schuster Adult Publishing Group.

The genetics of mood disorders, Tsuang, M.T. & Faraone, S.V., 1990. Baltimore, Md: Johns Hopkins University Press, cited in the National Institute of Mental Health *Fact Sheet on Bipolar Disorder Research*, 2004.

Useful Information On...PARANOIA, Revised by Margaret Strock, staff member in the Office of Scientific Information, National Institute of Mental Health, U.S. Department of Health and Human Services Publication No. (ADM) 89-1495, 2005.

We Heard the Angels of Madness: A Family Guide to Coping with Manic Depression, by Diane & Lisa Berger, Quill Press/ William Morrow & Company, New York, 1991.

Whispers: The Voices of Paranoia, by Ronald K Siegel, Simon & Schuster, 1996.

Acknowledgements

This book was written by numerous people. First, I am grateful to my late mother, Charlotte Reese, who modeled writing as a tenacious daily practice. After her death, along with copies of her columns for the *Reno Gazette-Journal,* I found her manuscript about the Callahan ranch, and a folder with news articles about my brother. These were valuable resources as well as the original inspiration for this book. I thank Milo for sharing thoughts—and some of the pain—about his illness. I am also grateful for the endorsement of my father, Oscar Reese, who felt that it would be helpful to others to hear our family story. My sister Carolyn helped with research and emotional support.. My husband Ted was patient throughout the process, always willing to read pages hot off the printer, and to give his discerning advice.

I owe many thanks to the staff at the Miami City Library, the people at the Reno City Library, and those at the Nevada State Library in Carson City. They guided me in research into the numerous newspaper articles about my brother's activities.

I appreciated the interviews with Michael Powell of the Federal Public Defender's office in Reno, George Flint, president of the Nevada Brothel Association, Dr. Randall Todd, State Epidemiologist for the Nevada Health Division, and Frank Mullen of the *Reno Gazette-Journal.* In Florida, Celeste Higgins, Federal Public Defender, Carol Collins of Paradise Aviation, and Steve Holstrom, with Tropical Fighters, were all generous with their time.

John Daniel, author, publisher, and friend, read the manuscript and offered many perceptive tips. His enthusiasm gave me the energy to go forward with this book.

I am indebted to my "sisters in writing" for their untiring support and helpful comments, especially Sharon Dirlam, Eleanor Jacobs, Kathy Hardin, Ann Ayres, Susan Eveler, Mara Kohn, Dr. Jan Rudestam, and Dr. Jeanette Webber.

And I am grateful to the late Bonnie Hill, who offered the idea for the title, *Solo Flight*. I regret that she did not live to see it in print.